Perfume
Dreams

Perfume Dreams

Reflections on the Vietnamese Diaspora

Andrew Lam

Foreword by
Richard Rodríguez

HEYDAY, BERKELEY, BALIFORNIA

Library of Congress Cataloging-in-Publication Data
Lam, Andrew.
Perfume dreams : reflections on the Vietnamese diaspora / Andrew Lam ; foreword by Richard Rodriguez.
    p. cm.
 Includes bibliographical references.
 ISBN 978-159714-020-1
1. Lam, Andrew. 2. Vietnamese Americans—Biography. 3. Lam, Andrew—Family. 4. Refugees—United States—Biography. 5. Vietnamese Americans—Social conditions. 6. Vietnamese Americans—Ethnic identity. 7. Vietnamese—Migrations. 8. Refugees—Social conditions. I. Title. E184.V53L36 2005
    305.895'92073'092—dc22

                    2005012942

Cover Photo: Khiem Do
Cover Design: Rebecca LeGates
Interior Design/Typesetting: Philip Krayna Design, Berkeley, CA

Orders, inquiries, and correspondence should be addressed to:
        Heyday
        P. O. Box 9145, Berkeley, CA 94709
        (510) 549-3564, Fax (510) 549-1889
        www.heydaybooks.com

10 9

For my parents

Contents

Acknowledgments

I am indebted to my friend, the author Richard Rodriguez, whose foreword graces this book. I owe my gratitude to William E. Justice, editor at Heyday, who saw a story in my various essays. I am also grateful to my friends Shawn, David, Kevin, Simon, Robin, Trung, Loan, and Milbert for their friendship and support over the years. To my sister Nancy, thanks for being a fan—even before I had any. I am inspired by Michael, who, despite his own sadness, struggles to do good in the world. To my cousin David, thanks for listening. Above all I would like to thank my colleague and friend, Sandy Close, executive editor of Pacific News Service, who sent me to travel the world.

Foreword
Richard Rodriguez

Andrew Lam is among the most cheerful people I have known. One is easily attracted to his nature as to sunlight. Some of Andrew's cheerfulness is discipline. Some of his humor is darkness.

Andrew Lam witnessed the fall of Saigon. What the child saw was that everything can fall down. His essays in this volume are about the consequences of tragedy, and sobriety is imposed upon them. But behind them, or behind Andrew, is some comic resolution to survive. That much I can say.

There is something puckish about Andrew—I mean this in precisely the Shakespearean sense—something impish, something sprightly, some goblin fascination with foolish mortality marks his regard. Puckish, too, in his relish of the world, and, once more, puckish in his contemplative aspect, his long, dispassionate regard of impermanence.

Some people who have seen what Andrew has seen would forswear humor or recoil from it thereafter. Andrew, however, has cultivated wit—repartee, sarcasm, irony, the writer's knowledge that words can be constructed so as to topple on cue. It may be that Andrew is comic in English, but not otherwise. Or is that even possible?

Andrew once told me of his affection for the adventures of Tintin, the French comic book hero. "When I am blue, I reread those stories in French, as I read them when I was a boy and dreamed of the world."

Tintin, an adolescent boy with a cresting curl on the top of his head, is a "famous reporter"; wears a trench coat; travels to exotic locales—to Russia, to the Congo, to Tibet, all beautifully rendered by the artist Hergé in a Japan-influenced style that is characteristically

French. Tintin takes with him his suitcase, his dog, Milou, and a salty sea captain.

You would think someone so violently separated from home by history would be forever in quest of a permanent address. But Andrew Lam craves movement. Perhaps it is a simple equation. Perhaps because his youth was characterized by impermanence, impermanence has come to represent youth.

In an essay on National Public Radio, Andrew described for listeners the occasion of his having to renew his American passport. The man of forty felt regret at relinquishing his old passport photograph, thus relinquishing the beauty of the twenty-year-old depicted there. Finally, the older man exchanges youth because he values more the boast of experience.

On the morning I write these words in California, Andrew is at a writer's conference in Sydney. A couple of months ago, he emailed a digital photograph of himself (alongside a distressed-looking camel) from North Africa. A few weeks after that, Andrew was on board United Airlines' inaugural flight from San Francisco to Saigon, the city the communists have renamed Ho Chi Minh City.

A few years ago, Andrew took an American television crew to his childhood home—an abandoned, shuttered, still-beautiful villa. Andrew's commentary for the film is Proustian in its consideration of fluid time, fluid nature, fluid history.

Along with various other complexities, Andrew Lam carries with him three languages: Vietnamese, French, English. He is nostalgic about French, which was, he says, "my real childhood language—my real childhood": "In a strange way, Vietnamese and English moved on with me to America, but French stayed behind in the villa and the garden of Dalat and the schoolyard of the Lycée Yersin."

In Andrew's memory there are haughty, aristocratic grandmothers, and there is—still neatly arranged on his bed—the blue uniform of his colonial education. There are servants. Courtyards. Limousines.

Andrew Lam's father was a high-ranking general in the South Vietnamese Army. Despite the privilege and comforts of the haute bourgeoisie that surrounded the family, Andrew knew his father was in constant danger. As Saigon fell, General Lam refused to abandon Vietnam unless, until, news of the South's surrender was announced on the radio.

Andrew did not know if he would see his father again when, on April 28, 1975, with his mother and sister and two grandmothers, Andrew fled Vietnam. He was eleven years old.

In the next panel, as in a comic book, Andrew is on the other side of the horizon. There are huge cumulus clouds and there is sunlight on a rayon wall—"a village of tents." He is in a refugee camp in Guam, eating a ham sandwich and drinking milk—"my first American meal."

After Guam, Tintin is transported to California, to an American junior high school. Andrew Lam is bewildered as well as bemused by the amiable chaos of the American classroom. After the formalities of the lycée, he finds himself faced with having to learn disrespect. It takes one year of American schooling for Andrew to learn to stop bowing to his teacher.

With the pleasure that is, as much as anything, his motif, Andrew will rehearse for you a lunatic lyric from his American childhood:

> My bologna has a first name,
> It's O-S-C-A-R;
> My bologna has a second name,
> It's M-A-Y-E-R.

Andrew learned American English from such ditties.

I can imagine the Lam family, newly arrived from Vietnam, in a northern California suburban house. Television fills the silence at dinner.

So different was this language of America—so glib, so loud—broadcasting "love" at every opportunity.

> Oh, I wish I were an Oscar Mayer wiener,
> That is what I'd really like to be.
> 'Cause if I were an Oscar Mayer wiener,
> Everyone would be in love with me.

"So different," Andrew remarks, "from all the chopstick cultures. My mother has never said to me, 'I love you.' Or, 'You are so dear to me.' Behavior is everything, not words. My mother tells me she loves me by cooking my favorite fish for dinner. And I express my love back to her by eating the fish."

During those high school years, Andrew lost his grasp on Vietnamese. Mouthfuls of consonants began to reform his tongue, his teeth, his lips. He became a confident speaker of American English. The most telling mark of his progress was this: "I was able to make kids laugh."

In college, Andrew began to think about writing. There was family precedent for taking up the artist's life. A poet-uncle survives in Hanoi. One of his grandfathers learned to play the violin in Paris "before coming home to die of an opium overdose at the age of thirty-four. Ah, there are so many things I cannot write in essays."

What things, Andrew?

"About ghosts. Sexuality. Religion. Unlike my fiction, my essays are not simply egotistical. They are written from a sense of responsibility."

When Andrew Lam began to write for a living, he wrote as a journalist—a journalist with literary flair. At Pacific News Service, Andrew filed a newspaper essay in which he rehearsed for readers his memory of the smell of barbequed dog. He believed he was writing securely within a Swiftian vein, but more swift was the disapproval of American readers.

One of my first memories of Andrew is of the young man I heard laughing over a reader's appalled response to that article. That was the first time I heard the laugh—the sublime, high-humored scorn of the monkey-god. There was no discernable humor in the young man's eyes. The sound was most like the defiant laughter of the child who has willfully tumbled a tower of blocks.

Andrew writes publicly only in English. He says, "When I started writing, it was never to the Vietnamese, but to the outsider." It is a difficult race to run, to be the first or among the first of one's Dewey-decimal kind to have a strong public voice.

But as he grew older, Andrew realized a responsibility to address a new generation of US-born Vietnamese who were without his memory of war and loss.

This generational distance strikes Andrew most forcefully when he returns to Vietnam and meets teenagers for whom the war—his war—is as distant as some grandfather's incoherent mumble: "I ask a teenager on the street of Saigon what she thinks of the war."

"Which war, Uncle?"

Andrew's favorite among Tintin's adventures is "Tintin au Tibet," wherein Tintin rescues a Chinese boy whose plane has crashed in the Himalayas.

"Reading out the dialogue of this story has such a calming effect on me. I feel connected to my childhood in Vietnam which, in turn, was connected, through Tintin, to a larger world."

So let us imagine Andrew Lam, the author of these essays, a citizen of that larger world, seeking the consolation of his childhood companion—the brave and resourceful Tintin, famous reporter, so far from home.

Lost Photos
October 1997

When I was eleven years old I did an unforgivable thing: I set my family photos on fire. We were living in Saigon at the time, and as Viet Cong tanks rolled toward the edge of the city, my mother, half-crazed with fear, ordered me to get rid of everything incriminating.

Obediently I removed pictures from the album pages, diplomas from their glass frames, film reels from metal canisters, letters from desk drawers. I put them all in a pile in the backyard and lit a match. When I was done, the mementos of three generations had turned into ashes.

Only years later in America did I begin to regret the act. A few pictures survived because my older brother, who was a foreign student, had taken them with him. But why didn't I save the rest the way I slipped my stamp collection in my backpack hours before we boarded the C-130 cargo plane and headed for Guam? For years I could not look at friends' family photo albums without feeling remorse.

Then last week I had a dream that was so instructive it left me with a different estimation of that loss. In the dream I find myself once more in front of my old home in Saigon. I walk through the rusted iron gate to find, to my horror, the place gutted—an empty structure where once there was life and love.

Immediately I start to rummage among the pile of broken bricks and fallen plasters, finding at last a nightstand that once belonged to my mother. I pull at its drawer and out spill dozens of black-and-white photos. I am ecstatic. The photos are intact.

They are exactly as I remember them. Here's one of my brother when he was twelve, wearing his martial arts uniform and bowing to the camera. Here's one of my mother as a teenager, posing next to the ruins of Angkor Wat. Here is my father as a young and handsome colonel, smoking a cigar. And me and my sister holding onto our dogs—Medor and Nina—as we wave to the photographer, smiling happily.

Suddenly a little boy appears in the dream. "This is my home," he yells, "and you're trespassing."

"But these are my photos," I meekly protest.

The boy looks at me with a mixture of suspicion and shrewdness and changes his tone. "Well," he says, "how much would you give me for these photos?"

But before I can find the answer, he laughs and snatches the photos out of my hand. I try to grab them back of course, but it's too late.

I woke to find my arm still reaching out over the blanket in a gesture toward the pictures, still trying to retrieve them. Confused, I stared at my own empty hand for what seemed to be a long, long time. In that salty dawn with the cable cars rumbling up and down the hills and their bells clanging merrily outside my window, I saw what I hadn't seen before: that nothing was ever truly lost.

What I failed to retrieve in the dream survives, if only as an exquisite longing. If words and language, as the poet Rilke tells us, can be made into a thing, mute as the statue of an orator, the reverse is true also.

Precious things lost are transmutable. They refuse oblivion. They simply wait to be rendered into testimonies, into stories and songs.

Child of Two Worlds
June 1998

> Two roads lead to my home: one long, yet short,
> the other short, yet long.
> > —from a Vietnamese folk song

Once, in my mother's garden in Dalat, Vietnam, I saw Mrs. Lau, the wife of our family servant, drag herself out of bed only a few hours after giving birth to bury her newborn's umbilical cord in our garden. Her gestures among the jasmine bushes, the mumbling of prayers, the burning of joss sticks, and the offerings of mangoes and rice stirred a deep sense of mystery in me. Later I asked my mother about the incident and she, in a solemn voice, announced that it was the Vietnamese way to ask the land to bless and protect the newborn. "Your umbilical cord is also buried in an earthen jar in our garden," she said. The incident and the knowledge of my own earthly ties made a strong impression on me: our ways were sacred and very old.

In that world of parochial sanctities, I was not entirely convinced that the outside world existed. Vietnam, the tropical garden, was all there was. Life was deemed cyclical but the world was not yet round. It hovered instead in my mind's eye in the shape of a voluptuous and ruffled S, the map of our country that I had more or less mastered in geography class in grammar school.

I remember standing in line before class with the others—white shirts and blue shorts, all—singing at the top of our lungs the national anthem each morning. "O Citizens, let's rise to this day of liberation," we would bellow. "Let's walk together and sacrifice our lives. Blood debt must be paid by blood." I had believed in the lyric, its every word, felt that shared patriotic fervor among my young,

3

bright-eyed peers. The war was at full throttle then, and we embraced it. In school we devised war games in which the winners would inevitably be Southerners, and the Northerners were often berated for trying to invade.

No Vietnamese history book, no patriotic song, no agrarian-based adage could have possibly prophesied my own abrupt departure from Vietnam nor my subsequent transnational ending. For at the end of the Vietnam War many of us did not die protecting river and land as we, in our rituals, games, poetry, and songs, had promised ourselves and our ancestors' spirits. For all the umbilical cords buried, for all the promises made, we did the unimaginable: we fled.

For the first time in Vietnam's embattled history, a history alleged to be four thousand years old, the end of a war had resulted in a mass exodus. A diaspora. Refugees, boat people, the dispossessed, three million Vietnamese or so scattered onto more than fifty countries across the globe.

On April 28, 1975, two days before Saigon fell to the communist army and the Vietnam War ended, my family and I boarded a cargo plane full of panicked refugees and headed for Guam. I remember watching Vietnam recede into the cloudy horizon from the plane's window, a green mass of land giving way to a hazy green sea. I was eleven years old.

I was confused, frightened, and from all available evidence—the khaki army tents in the Guam refugee camp, the scorching heat, the long lines for food rations, the fetid odor of the communal latrines, the freshly bulldozed ground under my sandaled feet—I was also homeless.

Places and times, when they can no longer be retrieved, tend to turn sacrosanct. Home forever lost is forever bathed in a certain twilight glow. Even after many years in America my mother still longed for the ancestral altar on which Grandpa's faded black-and-white photo stared out into our abandoned home. She missed the carved rosewood cabinet in which she kept the enamel-covered family albums and my father's special French wines from Bordeaux, and she yearned for the antique porcelain dining set covered by faded blue silk. She fretted over the small farm we owned near the Binh Loi Bridge on the outskirts of Saigon, where the chickens roamed freely and the mangosteen and guava trees were heavy with fruits when we last visited, and where the river, dotted with water hyacinths, ran swift and strong.

"This is the time of year when the guavas back home are ripened," Mother would tell the family at dinnertime.

So far from home, Mother nevertheless took her reference points in autumn, her favorite season. Autumn, the dark season, came in the form of letters she received from relatives and friends left behind. Brown and flimsy thin like dead leaves, recycled who knows how many times, the letters threatened to dissolve with a single tear. They unanimously told of tragic lives: Aunty and her family barely survived; Cousin is caught for the umpteenth time trying to escape; Uncle has died from heart failure while being interrogated by the Viet Cong; yet another Uncle is indefinitely incarcerated in a malaria-infested reeducation camp; and no news yet of Cousin and family who disappeared in the South China Sea. The letters went on to inquire as to our health and then to timidly ask for money, for antibiotics, for a bicycle, and, if possible, for sponsorship to America. The letters confirmed what my mother, who had lived through two wars, had always known: life is a sea of suffering, and sorrow gives meaning to life. Then, as if to anchor me in Old World tragedy, as if to bind me to that shared narrative of loss and misery, mother insisted that I, too, read those letters.

What did I do? I skimmed. I skipped. I shrugged. I put on a poker face and raked autumn in a pile and pushed it all back to her. "That country," I slowly announced in English, as if to wound, "is cursed."

That country, mind you. No longer mine. Vietnam was now so far away—an abstraction—and America was now so near (outside the window, blaring on TV, written in the science fiction books I devoured like mad)—a seduction. Besides, what could a scrawny refugee teenager living in America do to save Uncle from that malaria-infested reeducation camp? What could he do for Cousin and her family lost somewhere in the vast South China Sea? He could, on the other hand, pretend amnesia to save himself from grief.

My mother made the clucking sounds of disapproval with her tongue as she shook her head. She looked into my eyes and called me the worst thing she could muster: "You've become a little American now, haven't you? A cowboy." Vietnamese appropriated the word "cowboy" from the movies to imply selfishness. A cowboy in Vietnamese estimation is a rebel who, as in the spaghetti Westerns, leaves town, the communal life, to ride alone into the sunset.

Mother's comment smarted, but she wasn't far from the truth. Her grievances against America had little to do with the war and the United States' involvement in it. Her complaint against America was that it had stolen her children, especially her youngest and once most-filial son. America seduced him with its optimism, twisted his thinking, bent his tongue and dulled his tropic memories. America gave him freeways and fast food and silly cartoons and sitcoms, imbuing him with sappy happy-ending incitements.

Yet it could not be helped. For the refugee child in America, the world splits perversely into two irreconcilable parts: Inside and Outside.

Inside, at home, in the crowded apartment shared by two refugee families, nostalgia ruled. Inside, the world remained dedicated to What Was.

Remember the house we used to live in, with the red bougainvillea wavering over the iron gate? Remember when we went to Hue and sailed down the Perfume River for the night market and that night the sky was full of stars? Remember Tet, when Uncle showed us that trick with the cards?

Inside, the smell of fish sauce wafted along with the smell of incense from the newly built altar that housed photos of the dead—a complex smell of loss. Inside, the refugee father told and retold wartime stories to his increasingly disaffected children, reliving the battles he had fought and won. He stirred his whiskey and soda on ice, then stared blankly at the TV. Inside, the refugee mother grieved for lost relatives, lost home and hearth, lost ways of life, a whole cherished world of intimate connections, scattered and uprooted, gone, gone, all gone. And so Inside, I, their refugee child, felt the collected weight of history on my shoulders and fell silent.

Outside, however…

"What do you want to be when you grow up?" Mr. K., the English teacher in eighth grade, asked.

I had never thought of the question before. Such an American question. But it intrigued me. I did not hesitate. "A movie star," I answered, laughing.

Outside I was ready to believe, to swear that the Vietnamese child who grew up in that terrible war and who saw many strange, tragic, and marvelous things was someone else, not me, that it had happened in another age, centuries ago.

That Vietnamese boy never grew up; he wanders still in the garden of my childhood memory, whereas I—I had gone on. Hadn't I? It was a feeling that I could not help. I came to America at a peculiar age—pubescent, and not fully formed. Old enough to remember Vietnam, I was also young enough to embrace America, and to be shaped by it.

Outside, in school, among new friends, I spoke English freely and deliberately. I whispered sweet compliments to Chinese and Filipino girls and made them blush. I cussed and joked with friends and made them laugh. I bantered and cavorted with teachers and made myself their pet.

Speaking English, I had a markedly different personality than when speaking Vietnamese. In English, I was a sunny, upbeat, silly, and sometimes wickedly sharp-tongued kid. No sorrow, no sadness, no cataclysmic grief clung to my new language. A wild river full of possibilities flowed effortlessly from my tongue, connecting me to the New World. And I, enamored by the discovery of a newly invented self (I even gave myself a new name—"Andy, call me Andy," I would tell each new teacher and each new friend who had trouble pronouncing my Vietnamese name)—I sailed its iridescent waters toward spring.

Now, more than two decades later, in her suburban home with a pool shimmering in the backyard, my mother talks to ghosts. Every morning she climbs a chair and piously lights a few joss sticks for the new ancestral altar on top of the living room's bookcase and mumbles her solemn prayers to the spirits of our dead ancestors and to Buddha. On the shelves below stand my father's MBA diploma, my older siblings' engineering and business degrees, my own degree in biochemistry, our combined sports trophies, and, last but not least, the latest installments of my own unending quest for self-reinvention—plaques and obelisk-shaped crystals and framed certificates—my journalism awards.

What Mother's altar and the shelves carrying their various knickknacks seek to tell is the typical Vietnamese American tragicomedy, one where Old World Fatalism finally meets New World Optimism, the American Dream.

Almost half of Vietnamese moving abroad ended up in North America, and the largest portion of this population resettled in California. Vietnamese immigrants, within one and a half generations, have moved from living at the receiving end of industrial revolution to being players in the information age. The second largest Vietnamese population outside of Vietnam is centered around Silicon Valley.

Ours is an epic filled with irony: the most fatalistic and sentimental people in the world found themselves relocated to a state created by fabulous fantasies, high-tech wizardry, and individual ambitions.

My mother watches the smoke undulate before her eyes and sighs. Do her ancestors hear her prayers amidst this world of computers, satellite dishes, and modems? She does not know. But she does not like contradiction. One cannot be both this and that. She sees herself simply as a Vietnamese living in exile. She resists America as much as she can though she knows too well. She of sad-ending fairy tales, in her golden years, reluctantly concedes that she may have lost this battle with America. Spring will come.

In retirement my mother is a rejuvenated woman. She even goes to the gym with my father. She walks the treadmill religiously. Her fingers, fingers that once knew the blades of ripened rice and the gangrened wounds of dying soldiers, dart on the flat electronic panel of the cardio equipment at her spa with such ease. Mother even lifts weights.

All in all, she feels a little embarrassed that she still looks so young for a grandmother in her mid-sixties—her hair is jet black, her legs are sturdy, her arms strong, and there still echoes in her laughter that twang of the gaiety of the teenager. Her own mother at her age could barely walk. "If we were living in Vietnam now, I suppose I would sit on the wooden divan, fan myself, and chew betel nuts like your grandma."

To deny her own American conversion, Mother keeps a small garden. Lemongrass and mint vie for space among bitter melons, Vietnamese coriander *(rau ram)*, and basil. The air in the backyard is filled with scents of home. She insists on observing the death date of her father each year, complete with burning paper offerings and cooking a favorite dish for the dead. Each Tet, she stays awake all night to make Vietnamese rice cakes. And she tells Vietnamese stories, drenched in sadness, to anyone willing to hear.

Consider this then as a late Rockwell tableau: a sunny living room in a Silicon Valley home where a Vietnamese woman sits on her sofa, telling the story of an ill-fated princess to her two wide-eyed, American-born grandchildren.

Once, she says, there was a beautiful princess who fell in love with a fisherman who sang beautiful ballads of love each morning as he sailed past her pavilion. One day the fisherman, unaware of the princess's existence, sailed downriver to fish another kingdom. One season followed another and she, pining for his voice, fell ill and died. And in her ashes, in place of her heart, the king found a bright red ruby. He had it carved into a drinking bowl. And whenever he poured into it, the image of the fisherman appeared, sailing his boat on the water. And his voice is heard singing sweet and sad songs.

Years later, the fisherman came sailing back. He heard of this magic bowl and begged at the palace gate for entrance. Days passed and he despaired and began to sing. And his voice reached the king in his palace and the fisherman was summoned. Into the bowl, tea was poured. Then lo and behold, the fisherman watched in amazement as his own image appeared in the princess's heart. He began to weep. Had he only known of her love! Then another miracle: as one of his tears fell into the bowl, the bowl turned into blood and disappeared.

The story, taking its cue from a tradition of fatalism, does not go down well in America—certainly not with my brother's children. Back home children do not challenge such an outcome. Back home they accept that noble deeds are rarely rewarded with happily-ever-afters, that broken love is the norm, and that those who do good can be and often are punished. These stories are concerned with their young listeners' spiritual growth, not with convincing them that they live in a benevolent universe. Considering how the country has been war-ridden for thousands of years and how disasters have a way of destroying hope, Vietnamese tales have evolved to prepare the next generation for cataclysm and grief.

But my mother's grandchildren are Americans, are Californians, and they naturally resist her tragic endings. They challenge her fatalism with their American wisdom. "The princess only sleeps in the enchanted forest, Grandma. She waits for the Prince Charming kiss." My mother shakes her head and laughs. And she gives in. At her grandchildren's request, she slips in the video of *The Little Mermaid* and they watch the princess struggle toward a happily-ever-after.

What woke the Vietnamese refugee—that fleeing princess—from her millennial stupor, on the other hand, was no Prince Charming kiss but the simple yet potent idea of progression. A cliché to native-borns, the American Dream nevertheless seduces the sedentary Vietnamese to travel from halfway around the world. It's the American Dream that kissed her hard, tongued her, in fact, and in the morning she awakes to find, to her own amazement, that she can readily pronounce mortgage, escrow, aerobic, tax shelter, GPA, MBA, MD, BMW, Porsche, overtime, stock options. Gone is the cyclical nature of her provincial thinking, and lost is her land-bound mentality. She finds that she's upwardly mobile, that she is connected to other countries by virtue of her relatives spreading across the globe and by new communication technologies. She can email relatives as far away as France and Hong Kong. She can see the future.

She sees, for instance, her own restaurant in the "for rent" sign on a dilapidated store in a run-down neighborhood. She sees her kids graduating from top colleges. She imagines her own home with a pool in five years time—all things that were impossible back home. Indeed, she astonishes herself by her ambitions. We'll build a shop here, buy a house there. We'll borrow money and start a company in a few years if we work hard, really hard...

And why not? Her American Dream has chased away her Vietnamese nightmare. Compared to the bloody battlefields, the malaria-infested New Economic Zone, a vindictive communist regime that monitored everyone's movements, the squalid refugee camps scattered across Southeast Asia, the murders and rapes and starving and drowning on the high seas, California is paradise.

Soon enough houses are bought, jobs are had, children are born, old folks are buried, and businesses are opened. A community that previously saw itself as exiled, as survivors of some historical blight, as a people born from tragedy and who are prepared to return to their homeland, to tend their abandoned ancestral graves, to face their oppressors, slowly changes its mind. Its roots are sinking deeper and deeper into the American loam.

Soon enough in San Jose, Orange County, San Diego, LA (not to mention Houston and Dallas), up and down the California coast, Little Saigons, economic and cultural centers that altered the existing landscapes, begin to sprout and blossom. And the stories of the horrible war and terrifying escape over the high seas that once emanated from these places slowly give way to gossip of successes in the Golden Land.

Did you hear about the Vietnamese Rhodes Scholar in England? He was on the Tonight Show *with Johnny Carson.*

Brother, did you know that there is a Vietnamese astronaut at NASA?

Did you know that the first person to receive seven degrees from MIT was a Vietnamese boat person, and he did it in five years!

Remember him, Sister? He's now a CEO for a multimillion-dollar electronics firm in Silicon Valley.

The drama of the initial expulsion is replaced by the jubilation of a new-found status and wealth. Truth be told, the letters sent from Vietnam had far less a grip on my mother than the letters she, in turn, sent back home to those left behind. Full of reports of whose son and daughter graduated summa cum laude and valedictorian and whose husband has become a surgeon and whose wife has become a successful real estate agent and so on, and enclosed with photos of two-story homes, of expensive and shiny sports cars in front of which tall and beautiful children stand waving and smiling to the yokel cousins they barely remember, the letters confirmed for the long-suffering relatives back home what they have suspected all along: anything is possible in America.

A race of modern Ulysseses responded to my mother's siren letters. In the dead of night, Vietnamese bent on an American conversion climb on board—by the hundreds, by the thousands—old rickety fishing boats for the perilous journey to America.

Here then perhaps is the final irony of that bitter war: since the start of the Vietnamese Diaspora, when the war ended in 1975, Vietnam, having defeated imperialistic America, fell susceptible to America's charms and seduction. In their postwar poverty and suffering, Vietnamese yearned for a new beginning in America. They want Levi's, freedom, microwaves, democracy, double-tiered freeways, happiness. They diligently remove Uncle Ho's photo from their walls, and to replace the void they put up posters of *Baywatch* and AC/DC and Kiss. They slip a video from Hong Kong or Hollywood into the VCR and marvel at the beauty and glamorous possibilities that exist in the outside world.

What has happened is that a new and radical idea has injected itself in the Vietnamese land-bound imagination. It is a powerful migratory myth, one that exhorts fabulous cosmopolitan endings. And the Vietnamese language of nationalism, too—what had for millennia given the Vietnamese unfathomable strength to endure incredible suffering, to fend off foreign invaders and colonizers alike—has been subverted by a single vocabulary word: Viet Kieu.

Viet Kieu: Vietnamese nationals living abroad, especially those in America, whose successes and wealth serve as a mirror against which the entire nation, mired still in poverty and political oppression, reflects on its own lost potential. Uncle Ho Chi Minh once preached freedom and independence to his compatriots (though he meant independence and freedom from colonization and imperialism, not for the individual) to spur them to battle against the French and American and South Vietnamese. Today it is the Viet Kieu, those persecuted by Uncle Ho's followers and forced to flee—people like me—who exude that much-coveted independence and freedom.

"Go to America"—so goes the new Vietnamese mantra, where multiple reincarnations may be had in one lifetime. Go to America and your sufferings end. Go to America and your sons and daughters will grow up to be astronauts or presidents of rich computer companies.

It happened before. Surely it will happen again.

Trung, the rice farmer's son, for instance, the one who brought only seven oranges with him onto a crowded boat thinking they should last him the whole journey across the Pacific—how big is the ocean anyway?—had escaped to America. And instead of helping the old man plant next season's crop he turned into an architect who helps design—on his brand-new laptop—glassy high-rises for cities across the globe. And Thao, the jackfruit vendor's daughter who once expected to follow in her mother's footsteps, also escaped and found herself a decade or so later in a different kind of market: Wall Street. Now called Cynthia, a sophisticate, she is busy negotiating through her computer link-ups across time zones, oceans, continents.

And recently I read about a farmer who escaped Vietnam to become a well-known, successful businessman in the high-tech industry. He has returned to open shops in Vietnam. I could almost see the farmer turned high-tech entrepreneur as a character in some hybrid movie about Vietnam and America. In his high-rise, he sits staring down into the microchip on his finger and smiles; from certain angles at least, the tiny thing with its grids and lines that combines his ambition and his memories looks like a green, rich rice field, albeit portable and very, very small.

On the wall above my writing desk there's a photograph of me taken a few years ago during one of my many trips back to Vietnam as a journalist. In it I stand at the entrance of my old house; its green iron gates are rusted beyond recognition and the bougainvillea of my memory is gone.

Although I smile in the photo, it's a sad and discerning smile. For behind that smile is complex self-knowledge based on opposite ideas that took me a long, long time to grasp: the past is irretrievable yet I can never be free from it. Though I can never sever myself from my childhood visions and my own sentimental longings, I have irrevocably changed.

Somewhere in between the boy who once sang the Vietnamese national anthem in the schoolyard in Saigon with tears in his eyes and the man who writes these words was the slow but natural demise of the old nationalistic impulse. The boy was willing to die for his homeland. The man had become circumspect. The boy had believed that the borders, like the Great Wall of China, were real demarcations, their integrity not to be disputed. The man discovered that the borders have always been porous. The boy was once overwhelmed by the tragedy that had fallen on his people, had resented history for robbing him and his family of home and hearth and national identity. The man, though envious of the primacy of his childhood emotions, has become emboldened by his own process of individualization.

And yet this much is true also: were it not for my ties to the Vietnamese people, their trials and tribulations, were it not for my own memories of the life that was taken from me, my American individuality would be shallow.

Often I wonder why my Vietnamese childhood seems full of magic and why—though I am no longer beholden to the reality of my homeland with her many current troubles and problems—my memory of her continues to inform and inspire me. There are no easy answers to this, of course, but I think it has to do with that deep sense of reverence I once felt toward the land in which my umbilical cord is buried.

After all, to live in a less than modern society where land still holds your imagination, where ties are permanent, and where tradition is concrete, is, in a way, to live in an enchanted world. It's normal that your ancestors' ghosts talk to you in your dreams, that they inhabit all sorts of corners of your house, and that you should answer them in your prayers, in your offerings, in the incense smoke you burn nightly. In that world, omens are to be read from the wind, and the butterfly that comes hovering above the altar or lands on your shoulder is the spirit of your grandfather. On a certain day of the year, you do not leave the house for fear of bad luck; then on another the entire family flocks to the cemetery to burn offerings and cut the grass of Grandpa's grave to appease him in the spirit world.

Which is to say Vietnam was once for me a world full of deep mystery and I lived then in awe of the hallowed land, its powers.

And then no more.

The greatest phenomenon in this century, I am now convinced, has little to do with the world wars but with the dispossessed they sent fleeing; the cold war and its aftermath has given birth to a race of children born "elsewhere," of transnationals whose memories are layered and whose biographies transgress national boundaries.

Globalization for me means, among other things, a world awash with people whose displaced lives mock the idea of borders. They are prophets of migration, moving from language to language, sensibility to sensibility, constantly in flux, shifting. And if the Vietnamese refugee left Vietnam under the shadow of history, he also, in the blink of an eye, became the first global villager by default. The trauma of his leaving, the effort he makes in claiming and creating a new place for himself in a quickly shifting world, his ability to negotiate himself in an age of open systems and melting borders makes him the primary character in the contemporary global novel.

My sense of home these days seems to have less to do with geography than imagination and memories. Home is portable if one is in commune with one's soul. I no longer see my identity as a fixed thing but something open-ended. What lies before me then is a vision of continents overlapping and of crisscrossing traditions. Call it a new American frontier if you will, but one chased by a particular transpacific sensibility. For mine is a landscape where Saigon, New York, and Paris intersect, where the Perfume River of Hue flows under the Golden Gate Bridge.

I applaud Edward Said, the cultural critic who suggests that if one wishes to transcend his provincial and national limits, one should not reject attachments to the past but work through them. Irretrievable, the past must be mourned and remembered and assimilated. To truly grieve the loss of a nation and the robbed history of a banished people, that old umbilical cord must be unearthed and, through the task of art, through the act of imagination, be woven into a new living tapestry.

Trung, the farmer turned architect, knows something of this. Perhaps that is why he paints late at night. On his large canvasses, blurred figurines amid a sea of colors dance, mourn, contemplate, or simply gawk at the stars. What Trung knows but cannot say is that some psychic disconnection occurred the moment he left the rice field to embrace a new cosmopolitan reality. Yet something survived. Call it restlessness of the soul. And though he designs homes and condos by day, at night he paints like a demon.

Another friend, a poet who left Vietnam at age seven, tells me his unfinished book of poetry is his true home. It is the only thing he takes with him as he travels. I've read his poems. They are dark and lyrical yet void of rancor. They range instead like clouds or rain as to create a new space—his words are to replace lost land—for all displaced souls to dwell.

And me—each morning I write. I long for freedom. I yearn for memory. And only this morning as I type these words does it occur to me that mine too, strangely enough, is a kind of filial impulse, an effort to reconcile between spring and autumn, between my agricultural past and my cosmopolitan future.

Still, I shudder at the irony. The sounds of my fingers gliding on the keyboard remind me of the solemnity of my mother's morning prayers. When I was younger, I found Mother's story of the weeping fisherman and his dead princess morbid—so much death and blood and sorrow seem to plague the Vietnamese narratives, even those told to children. Only now, approaching middle age, do I recognize that the sad tale is, in its own wise way, one of requited love.

"Tell me, where are you from?" the platinum blonde in a black Donna Karan dress asked me at a recent cocktail party in a Russian Hill villa.

I gestured my martini to the shimmering bay outside the French window and smiled. "Over there, long ago."

"Oh!" she said. She did not know what to make of such an opaque answer or how to reconcile the sadness in my voice with the gesture and the smile. What I was not willing to divulge at such a festive event is that somewhere in between "here" and "over there" a part of me ceased to exist.

In my mind now, I see him as if in a newsreel. See him standing on the beach in Guam at sunset, a small boy staring westward, the waves lapping at his feet, tears in his eyes. A day after Saigon fell and he is alone. See him raise his hand, reluctantly, shyly, and wave good-bye to that S-shaped land. He waves some more, as if somehow this overzealous gesture will alleviate his sorrow. But then his eyes begin to wander. He notices the glowing soda pop machines by the army PX with all the choices—Coca-Cola, Pepsi, Dr. Pepper. He is mesmerized by their colorful glow, so beautiful and entrancing. He is awed. Then he hears two young GIs joking with one another as they stroll toward their sports car. He grows curious about the language of the young men. It's full of laughter and banter, a seductive song to his ears. He feels his tongue curling inside his mouth, forming new words, new names of things. His eyes follow them as they drive out of the refugee camp down the smooth freeway. The sun is almost gone now, a tiny golden arc over a darkening sea. On the red sand, the boy's shadow elongates. He turns then, toward the open road. Takes a step. Then another. And the sun disappears entirely. And he, too, is gone.

Into memories.

Into words.

Letter to a Young Refugee
April 1999

On the news last night I saw you amidst a sea of desperate Albanian refugees and afterward I couldn't get the image out of my mind. You with your wide eyes and shy smile, your hand gripping your mother's as if it were a lifesaver, you are repeating my story of a few decades ago.

Listen, even if I know so little about your country's tumultuous history, even if I don't know your name, I think I know what you are going through. When I was eleven, about your age, I too fled from my homeland with my mother and sister and two grandmothers when the communist tanks came rolling into Saigon, Vietnam. We ended up in a refugee camp while our father was left behind.

Back then I couldn't make any sense out of what had happened to me or my family. History, after all, is always baffling to the young. One day I am reading my favorite comic book in my mother's garden, my two dogs sleeping lazily at my feet, and the next day I am running for my life with a small backpack in which I only managed to save my stamp collection. Everything else was burnt— photographs, mementos, books, toys, letters, identifications.

For the first few days in the refugee camp I walked about as if in a kind of trance. I kept thinking I would return home. I kept thinking this was just camping and soon my father would rescue us, would take us home to what I knew and loved. I had no words, no references to what I was experiencing. But now I know: I was dispossessed, an exile.

My young friend, there are so many things I want to tell you, so many experiences I want to share with you, but most of all I want to warn you that the road ahead is a very difficult and treacherous one and you must be brave, strong, and cunning. There are crucial things you should learn and learn quickly and then there are things you must mull over for the rest of your life.

The immediate thing is to learn to rise as early as possible. The food line is always long, and no matter how early you are, there will always be a line. You must have a hat or a scarf to protect your head from the cold and then from the sun.

When you get to the end of the line, try to act as helpless and as sad as possible. Tell the person in charge of food that your frail grandmother is bedridden and could not wait in line, that you are feeding her. Cry if you can. Try not to feel ashamed. That you never begged before in your life means nothing. Swallow your pride. Another plate will save you or your mother or sister many hours of waiting for the next meal. It will give them time to stand in line for medicine or clothes, if there are any.

Listen carefully, a new reality is upon you and you must rise to it as best you can. It entails a drastic change in your nature, in your thinking. It requires new flexibility and courage. Be aggressive even when you are naturally shy. Be brave even though until recently you still hugged your teddy bear in your own bed going to sleep.

Be fierce. Do not let others take advantage of you. Do not show that you are weak. In the worst circumstances, the weak get left out or beaten and robbed. Arm yourself if you can—a knife, a stone—and guard your family and what possessions you have left like a mad dog its bone. People can sense that you are willing to fight for what you have and most will back away.

Be alert. Listen to gossips and news. Find out what is coming down the line: food, donated clothes, blankets, tents, medicines. Always get more than you need if you can manage it because what you have extra can be traded with others for something you don't have or can be given away to the elderly and feeble who are not as quick as you. An extra blanket is so helpful on a cold spring night, as you, I'm sure, have already found out.

Be hopeful. Maybe your father has made it somewhere else, to another camp possibly. The same can be said of your aunts and cousins, friends and neighbors. Never give up hope. Soon enough the camp will organize and there'll be a newsletter with information regarding lost relatives looking for each other or there'll be a bulletin board with names and agencies that will track displaced loved ones. Go every day to check to see whether your father has sent word. Console your inconsolable mother and sister. Hug them as often as you can.

My young friend, I close my eyes now and cast my mind back to that time spent in the refugee camp and all I hear are the sounds of weeping. I imagine it is not that different from what you are hearing now each morning, each afternoon, each night. Throughout the green tent city that flapped incessantly in the wind was the music of sorrow and grief. A woman who saw her husband shot in front of her wailed until she was hoarse and breathless. A man who left his feeble father behind cried quietly into his blanket. A woman whose teenage son was lost in the escape stared out into the dark as if she had lost her mind. For a while, the sound of weeping was my refugee camp lullaby.

Life in limbo is difficult and humiliating, but you must remember that being robbed of what you loved does not speak to your weakness or frailty. It only speaks of the inhumanity and fear and hatred of those who caused you to flee and endure in this new dispossessed reality.

I implore you, do not give in to their hatred. I know it is very hard, if not impossible, for someone who has just been forced out of his homeland, but you must try. Those who killed and robbed and caused so much pain and suffering to you, your family, and your people are, in fact, trying to make you into their own image, even if they don't realize it yet. They want you to hate just like them. They want you to be consumed with the fire of their hatred.

But don't hate. It will take great strength not to hate. And it will take even greater resilience to not teach hatred to those who come after you. Hatred consumes oppressed and oppressors alike and its terrible expressions—revenge is chief among them—always result in blood and tears and injustice and unspeakable suffering, an endless cycle of grief.

Learn to love what you have instead, learn to love those who suffered along with you, for their suffering and yours are now part of your inheritance.

Above all, don't forget. Commit everything—each blade of grass, each teary-eyed child, each unmarked grave—to memory. Then when you survive and are older, tell your story. Tell it on your bruised knees if you must, tell it at the risk of madness, scream it from the top of your lungs.

For though the story of how you suffered, how you lost your home, your loved ones, and how you triumphed is not new, it must always be told. And it must, by all means, be heard. It is the only light we ever have against the overwhelming darkness.

Notes of a Warrior's Son
February 2005

I am approaching the age my father was when he came here to America from Vietnam at the end of the war. It doesn't matter that I have been making a living as a commentator and journalist for more than a dozen years; I'm struggling to write down these words, what I need to tell about a war that is long over, yet hasn't, in many ways, ended. It continues to divide as well as claim us.

Once, a long time ago in South Vietnam, my father was a proud general, a warrior fighting in a civil war that lasted more than a quarter of a century. As a child born in the middle of that war, I had looked up to a man who seemed more like a deity than a father. Hadn't I imagined myself as an adult walking in his soldierly footsteps?

But then it all changed.

Near the end of the war, when ammunitions were dwindling and soldiers had to ration bullets and helicopters were grounded, and with American support long gone, president Nguyen Van Thieu ordered many of South Vietnam's commanders from the four military regions to pull back troops and protect the larger vicinity of Saigon, leaving the rest of the country vulnerable to the invading communist army.

My father, Thi Quang Lam, was a lieutenant general, commander of an army corps task force along the Demilitarized Zone that divided Vietnam in two. Since there were no retreat plans, he resisted at first, arguing that retreating without a clear plan of action would cause many deaths, and besides, attacks from the North hadn't been so intense there as they were elsewhere. But his superior commander in Danang ordered a retreat the second time, citing executive orders, and my father relented.

Father and his troops boarded naval ships in Hue and came back to Danang, fifty miles to the south. Then, a few days later, when Danang fell, they boarded ships to Vung Tau, a coastal town east of Saigon.

I saw him then. Father was a changed man. Gone was the regal and cold demeanor of the three-star general whose presence once struck fear in others. There was agitation in his eyes and he was deathly ill. I hadn't seen him in such a state before and it sent chills up and down my spine. If Father, who I worshipped and believed to be fearless and powerful, were distraught and rendered helpless, what would become of the rest of us?

In Vung Tau, Father received orders to turn himself in. He and six other generals were under arrest. Their crime: withdrawing troops without executive orders. Read: so many displaced soldiers and displeased generals in one area could spell a military coup, so President Thieu was preventing that potential uprising even as his empire was, due to the advancing communist army, dwindling to a fourth of its previous size.

While the military commanders languished in jail and the lower-ranking officers tried to hold their restive military personnel together, Thieu fled the country, to be followed by those who could afford it and those with high connections overseas. A week or so after Thieu left, my father and the other generals were released from jail.

A few days after that and the war was over. It ended on April 30, 1975, when communist tanks rolled into Saigon and one in particular crashed dramatically through the gilded gates of the Independent Palace while helicopters carrying refugees fled to waiting naval ships.

On that morning, Father left Vietnam. Upon news that the South Vietnamese government had surrendered, he boarded a ship with a few hundred other Vietnamese officials and their families on the Saigon River and headed out to sea. Nearing Subic Bay in the Philippines where they asked US authorities for asylum, he folded away his army uniform, changed into a pair of jeans and a shirt, and, now a stateless man, tossed his gun into the water.

I was not there. I was already in Guam, having left inside a humming cargo plane full of panicked refugees out of Tan Son Nhat

Airport two days before Saigon fell. I remember huddling next to my mother, older sister, and two grandmothers, sporadically watching Vietnam recede from the horizon through the plane's window. My next memory is of eating an impossibly delicious ham and cheese sandwich in a hangar of a US air base.

Though I did not bear witness to Father's gesture, I can see it clearly, having imagined it over the years. I see his hand trembling before he flings the gun out in an arc over the sea, which rises to swallow it. I see his eyes looking to the water as he thinks about an uncertain future in exile, the wind sending his white shirt to billow. I was not there to witness it, but I've come to regard that moment when he jettisoned his gun into the sea as a major turning point in my own story. That gun, rusting at the bottom of the sea, serves as a kind of marker. It spelled the end of my childhood mythology.

Our first home in America was a crowded two-bedroom apartment near the end of Mission Street, where San Francisco ended and the suburbs began. My aunt and her four children and my older brother, a foreign student boarding with them, were already living there, and there was little space to be had. We slept where we could: under the breakfast table, on cots and couches, three to a bed.

My aunt had been struggling. Married to a Vietnamese career diplomat who had abandoned her, she ran a small restaurant downstairs to make ends meet. We all pitched in but it was difficult going. It did not help that we were still in profound shock.

We received no news of Father when we were in the refugee camp in Guam, nor did we know of his fate when we first came to America. My mother, who looked haggard, whose eyes were hollow and red from crying each night since we left Vietnam, didn't say anything but we could tell what was on her mind. Father could have stayed behind. Father could have, out of patriotism and loyalty to his men, rejoined them and fought on somewhere regardless of the outcome. Besides, we all knew he hated losing and that honor dictated that most-drastic action of all among the men of his generation: *tu thu.* Other generals had committed suicide when their outposts were overrun by communist forces. I had heard my mother whisper these words to my aunt one night, and afterward I couldn't go to sleep. *Tu thu*: defending to the death. *Tu thu, tu thu,* the words echoed ominously in my head.

But then one afternoon at the restaurant the phone rang. Mother picked it up. On the other end was Father's voice. She gasped. She cried. She was speechless. She recovered herself and laughed. They didn't talk long but when she hung up she and my aunt hugged each other. I watched from the kitchen counter as the two women wept in the manner of people who have been struggling to stay afloat at sea for a long time and suddenly see a ship on the horizon. It was only when I saw my mother happy again that it occurred to me what it was that we had experienced since we left Vietnam: despair.

A dark cloud lifted. That night I heard the adults laugh. It was so rare that it felt as if we were living in Vietnam again during the festive days of Tet. My family was talking all at once. We smiled. We joked. We talked about having a party to welcome Father to his new home. We were no longer shadows flitting about in the dank and dark apartment. I remember walking about, trembling with joy and anticipation. Father was coming. We would be whole again, restored to our nobility once more, wouldn't we?

For a while inside that crowded apartment my father, the exiled general, brooded. He read newspapers but hadn't moved toward finding a job. He drank every evening and watched TV. I would sidle up to him and sit on his lap, and father and son would cuddle like we used to in Vietnam. He would absentmindedly rub my hair, kissed my cheek and let me hug him. But I was growing up very fast, my voice had begun to change, and though I remember being next to him, I also felt that something was amiss. He was going through the gestures but his eyes were staring at things that were not in that living room. On the old black-and-white TV, Walter Cronkite was telling us of the horror of postwar Indochina: boat people dying on the high sea, Cambodia disappearing under Khmer Rouge control, and so on. Father responded to all the bad news by making a low, throaty sound as if he were a caged animal, "Huh! Huh!"

Late at night in the privacy of their own room my parents argued. My mother—who had waited near the end of the war on the beach of Danang under an umbrella for Father's naval ship to dock from Hue while communist mortars fell from the Hai Van Pass onto the city behind her, killing hundreds—my mother—who showed the kind of loyalty that could easily be glorified in any Confucian parables—now threatened to leave him if he wouldn't shape up. "A three-star general's wife is now a short-order cook. Why is not her husband working as something, anything?" Mother shouted. Did he want to see his children starve to death in America, she asked?

I don't remember Father's response or if, in fact, he'd said anything at all, besides telling her to keep it down. I remember, however, my two grandmothers shaking their heads and counting their rosaries in the living room, pretending not to hear. What happened to the brave, brilliant, handsome husband and father and exemplary son? Who was this quiet man who, at forty-three, only talked when he drank?

Outside the window, across the street, in the supermarket parking lot, my brother was a lone figure in semidarkness. He swept and cleaned, a janitor making very little money. He'd left Vietnam a prince. He didn't flee as a refugee like the rest of us, but history had caught up with him just the same and turned him into a pauper. So he withdrew into himself and moped. My brother, who had adored and worshipped my father, who had accompanied him even to the war zones by helicopter when he was young and served as Father's map bearer, and who had worked extremely hard to earn a black belt in tae kwon do at the age of twelve in order to please him, became impossible in America. He talked back. He slapped me around on occasion. He fluctuated between obedient son and brooding teenager, between wanting to be a hero in a lost war and wanting to rebel against fate. He would some nights come home drunk and add to the growing fire of familial discontent.

Secretly the rest of the family had nursed a fantasy: Father would somehow restore us to the glory of an upper-class life. We were not fully prepared to accept our new reality—how could we? Nor could we accept that Father was himself helpless, that he was in a state of profound shock and was haunted by the deaths of so many. That he had demons of his own.

It would take almost two years for his demons to release some of their hold on him so that he could begin to remake himself, to move us into a middle-class life, to obtain, in what seemed like a Herculean task, an MBA through night school while working at the bank as a trust officer. But by then the love and respect and filial piety that insulated and gave structure to our family had cracked and waned, and America and all of its allures had seeped in, dividing us, redefining us, such that we were becoming strangers to one another.

A baccalaureate in French philosophy, a reader of Camus and a fan of La Fontaine, a third-degree black belt in tae kwon do, a warrior and philosopher, Father was supposed to be at the top of his game. In Vietnam, because of his many victorious battles and his dark skin, the Viet Cong called him "the Black Panther of the South," a rare compliment. But the theater in which he had held center stage was now gone, swept away right from under his army boots. In America he was restrained, frustrated, and, for a while, without direction. In America all he owned were his memories, and in time they began to own him.

Never a bad drunk, his silence would nevertheless give way to a loud, booming voice that told stories of the battles he had fought and won. My aunt and her four children had moved out by then, only to be replaced by another aunt, the youngest of three sisters, and her family. The new aunt worked in the same restaurant with her sisters while the two brothers-in-law began the ritual of reminiscing. My youngest aunt's husband was a paratrooper captain in the South Vietnamese Army. He had seen his fair share of bloodshed. Often he would join Father for drinks in the evening and the two living room warriors would compare battle scars, recalling the brave and stupid things they did as soldiers, as young men.

I remember in Sa Dec when the Viet Cong attacked our home...

I remember going up in Cambodia that year when we invaded. Nearly got killed...

I remember parachuting down in the middle of a minefield...

This way each night the war came back. In our dilapidated living room the sounds of B-52 bombs echoed, napalm burst forth over thick jungle canopies, helicopters landed in fertile rice paddies.

Many times I would close my eyes and listen. I remember our helicopter flight over flooded rice fields late one night from Quang Tri back to Hue, and how a perfect yellow moon was racing in the watery paddies below us, one square after another. I remember standing with pride in the VIP stand next to Father as we watched a military parade in Dalat. And one night as he talked about Hue I saw myself again by the Perfume River, waiting for Father's helicopter to land, the tall elephant grass wavering. When he was on the ground I ran rushing into his arms and he laughed as he lifted me up for a warm embrace.

Father's kisses were full of stubble and his wet uniform emitted the smell of sweat, cologne, mud, cigars, and gunpowder—smells that I will always associate with the battlefield. I was happy in that embrace, happy near that ancient river named for the fragrance of lotus blossoms that bloomed in late summer; it flowed like history itself, at times fast and furious, at others gentle and calm, and until then still on our side...

When I opened my eyes again and looked around, I saw a very different world: two men sitting on a worn-out couch under a dim light, talking about what was lost and gone, the TV showing Carol Burnett aping Tarzan, a faded poster of the Golden Gate Bridge on the wall, ragged curtains, and, out the window, the L&M supermarket with its working-class shoppers and the fog drifting— my cold and somber new world.

Father kept talking. His drunken voice shook every pane of glass in our new home, stirred every mote of dust, and filled me, slowly but surely, with a sense of doom. His defeat, my legacy; his bitterness, my inheritance.

His voice had once caused his soldiers to tremble. In America, however, it turned into a voice that gradually struck me as nostalgic and, despite its bravado, full of regrets. When drunk he exuded a certain kind of childlike excitement and, slurring, he would repeat certain words over and over again for emphasis, and his booming laughter over some event or another could be deafening. Forceful and loud, his voice nevertheless began to sound like an overture to unrequited longing.

Father never talked of losing, never talked of how horrific the evacuation had been, of how seasick he was, needing help climbing that ship from Hue to Danang during the retreat and then from the ship to shore, nor how he was sick all the way back to Vung Tau. Mother did. Others, including the aide-de-camp who left Vietnam with him and became an engineer in San Jose, did. As did the captain of the ship who took him from Danang to Vung Tau, who saw people—panicked civilians—chopped to pieces by the departing ships' rudders. The naval captain became a real estate agent in Fremont but remained forever haunted by what he had seen. Whenever he visited our family and was sufficiently drunk, he couldn't stop talking about it.

The obvious gradually dawned on me as it must have struck my older brother much earlier on—that, in America, the warrior's glorious beginning had twisted into an ignoble end. Our side lost, we became exiles, enemies of history. That despite his penchant to tell war stories in the evening, restoring lost glory, it was no longer within his power to restore any one of us, least of all himself, to the nobility that was once his. Father, who was born into a wealthy land-owning family in the Mekong Delta, had spent the first half of his life living and making history, and he was now spending his second half in exile reliving it.

But that past, one that borders on the mythic, could not provide my brother, sister, and me any road map in America, our new home. What is epic in one country is inconsequential in another. Vietnamese have no real biographies in the American narrative, no real history. Invisibility, it seemed, was our fate.

If Father was a defeated warrior, who was I? If he was on the loser's side of history, whose side was I on? Back in Vietnam I was someone who lived in the center of an ongoing saga, surrounded by servants and soldiers, someone whose father could call thunder down from the sky; in America I was a lonely refugee child whose story is but a footnote in the public consciousness. Vietnamese are faceless in Vietnam War movies in America. Vietnamese wear conical hats and die shouting as blood spurts from their torsos on the silver screen. The three-sided war where North and South fought against one another with the Americans as allies to the South turned into a much simpler version in America. In the movies—in the popular

imagination—the narrative often told is that of an American protag-
onist in a foreign land, under siege, fighting all faceless Vietnamese.

What is one to do then in such a world, one that has few reference
points to his own past, his own memories, his own existence?

I, the youngest child, who had wanted to believe that I could
find glory in my father's war stories, who had, like my brother,
fantasized a heroic life for myself in fighting that war too, brooded.
My voice barely broken, I had already become a bitter veteran of a
war that I had never actually fought.

My first act of betrayal.

A year or so had passed. Another general, a close friend of the
family, visited us. My father wanted my brother to come downstairs. They had had many fights by then, and a gap had widened
between them, a void filled with silence and resentment. Yet if
there was an unwritten familial contract between us all it was one
that said "One must not lose face to visitors, to outsiders." Father,
in a rare happy mood, insisted that I go upstairs to retrieve my
brother. My brother was ironing his shirt to go out. He said, "Tell
the old man I am not going down."

"You won't obey Father's words?" I asked in Vietnamese, incredulous.

"Tell him I don't give a damn about his words."

If I was shocked and offended, secretly I was also thrilled. How
daring! His disobedience had never risen to this level before, and it
impressed me as much as it offended my Confucian sensibilities.

"You sure that's what you want me to say?"

"Yes."

In front of my aunt and her husband, in front of my mother and
father's colleague, someone who respected him a great deal and he
likewise, I repeated my brother's line to Father, word for word.

Father's face dropped, his eyes narrowed. He looked not angry,
exactly, but rather miserable. His friend pretended not to hear but
there was a hush in the restaurant, followed by Mother's high-
pitched wail. It was after hours, thank god, but it was bad enough. I
was promptly told to leave. Then my older sister, who was working
in the kitchen, was sent to fetch our brother and she slapped me on
the way down. Hard.

"You don't know what you did, do you?" she screamed through tears. "You just shamed our entire family."

Did I know tact? Why did I not lie to protect my father? My brother? My family's honor?

Perhaps in some way I did know. Perhaps in my own way I had wanted to test the limits of familial disobedience.

There was yelling downstairs. I sat upstairs and fretted. More shouting, then, abruptly, silence. A slap? A hit on the head? I never knew. Never found out. A few minutes later, my brother came back up. His face was red, eyes full of tears. Anything could have happened. He could have been yelled at by my father or slapped by my mother or both. Surely he was shamed in front of our distinguished guest. Although I expected it, he did not hit me.

"I won't punish you," he said, glaring at me. "But you had better watch yourself from now on."

I, who had once adored my brother back in Vietnam, could see the hatred in his eyes. That hatred was met, alas, in mine.

Here is what the thesaurus has to offer for the not-so-common American term "unfilial": aweless, undutiful, bad-mannered, blasphemous, bold, cheeky, contemptuous, discourteous, flip, flippant, fresh, ill-bred, ill-mannered, impertinent, impious, impolite, impudent, insolent, irreverent, misbehaved, nervy, profane, rude, sacrilegious, sassy, saucy, smart-alecky, snippy, uncivil, ungracious.

The rude, impious son. The selfish kid. Blabbermouth. Traitor. That was what I was called at various times by various members of my own family and extended family and family friends. Over the years their whisper became a kind of poem.

He's not Vietnamese!
So American, a cowboy.
How quickly he changed!
Can't trust him: he
opposes his father.

Even now I've found it almost an impossible task to talk about the tragedy in the lives of those who emerged from the horror seemingly unscathed. Among those who suffered far worse, amidst a community formed by calamity and unspeakable losses, my family is considered very lucky. People had lost loved ones to the war, to the reeducation camps, to the New Economic Zones, to the Thai pirates, to thirst and starvation over the high sea. We came early, among the first wave. We survived as a unit intact. Many came later, after years of languishing in refugee camps. So—we internalized our losses instead, my family and I, and grieved alone.

An otherwise seemingly smooth trajectory toward a middle-class life in America was marred by familial discontent. The old values no longer held. Bickering became our habit, arguments erupted daily, but I, the youngest, fell silent. And my silence, I think, hurt my parents more than my brother and sister's discords. At least they were interacting. They fought but they stayed around, engaged. They both went to college while living at home. I, on the other hand, was, at an earlier age, plotting my escape.

I had grown to resent my entire family, but especially my own father. His memories, his stories were powerful. Repeated, they became lore, and they had begun to exert their terrible powers over him. Worse, they were beginning to snare me as well.

For despite his French education and his willingness to work hard, he had no idea what my life was like outside of the house. His only way to measure anyone and anything was in relation to the war, to the past, to his position as a respected general and warrior, and this was how he held himself in America, which is to say overtly proud, contemptuous of the world and, unless he was drinking, cold and aloof.

Yet the past was dividing us, and Father did not see it. He saw himself as a political exile and had no need to question his identity whatsoever. As his children it was understood that we were to accept that exile identification for ourselves as well. His interactions with Americans were all out of necessity; he claimed none of them as his friends. But a Vietnamese general living in exile in America at least knew where he stood in relation to history. His identity, even if ignominious, was assured. In war, after all, there are winners and there are losers.

As a Vietnamese community began to form around him and its culture of nostalgia defined the communal ethos, Father was becoming once more a visible icon of an unfinished war. Its extra-territorial passion gave rise to a new sensibility in the Little Saigons sprouting up and down the California landscape and across the United States, and it was one that dwelled on tragedy and grief. To be a fully active part of this community, members mourn, protest, and, on occasion, gather en masse to demand a communist-free homeland. In this society, Father was a VIP, a guest at political rallies, an engaging speaker during Tet festivals, a symbol of lost heroism. I once saw him on a dais on the fairground in Santa Clara speaking with passion, his audience in rapt attention. He was spurring the collective to continue on with the good fight against their mortal enemy—the communist regime—even if only in thoughts and words.

But what about his teenage son?

I was growing up with two very different ideas of history, two sets of civilizations, two traditions, two languages, two sets of behaviors, and I was, for what seems now a long, long time, floundering between them.

There was Vietnam, its cast of exiles whose sorrow and losses held them in many ways beholden to the past. Theirs is a history that runs seemingly backward. Their life in America has no special meaning, no great implications. They only remember what was robbed from them, what was lost. History for Father, and for those men who still wear their army uniforms at anticommunist rallies decades after the war ended, has a tendency to run backward, to memories of the war, to a bitter and bloody struggle whose end spelled their defeat and exile. And it holds them static to a lonely nationalism stance. They live in America but their souls are in Vietnam.

The history of the defeated is private and circular. It binds us all at the core, it is the ball and chain around a prisoner's bleeding ankle. In it, the only moral direction to be had is the one that demands complete loyalty to the past—not to own it, mind you, but to let oneself be ruled by it, and to do so one has to accept forever the status of a stranger in a strange land.

Then there was America. Its narrative is a forward arc and it encourages self-invention. In America one feels little the weight of history. The past is not important; the future is always bright.

America approves of amnesia, spurs the separation between children and parents, assumes the premise of ever expanding opportunities. Americans say, I need my own space. An individual is successful when, so the expression goes, he comes into his own. America offers redemption at the end of the road and, for the newcomer, a marvelous transformation of the self: a rebirth.

As a teenager I intrinsically understood that in order to have any control in my own life, I had better embrace the second narrative and go down that road as fast and as furiously as I could, wherever it would take me. And in order to do so, I must act for myself and, more important, think for myself.

For a Vietnamese child who was once ruled by rigid Confucian mores there is nothing so thrilling yet fraught with guilt as learning to disobey. He sees that his parents are fallible. He learns that, in fact, he is a better navigator in the New World where his parents, clinging desperately to the past, to traditional values to guide them, fumble and lurch and retreat into smallness—private world, private community, private cultures, private memories, private sorrows.

The immigrant child, wanting the larger world, shunning the old ways, inexorably breaks his parents' hearts.

"So are you sad you lost the war?" Remigio, my best friend from high school freshman year, asked. American-born, he was wide-eyed for war stories. He was in awe of my exotic beginnings, of my father's quiet presence in the living room listening to the news. Remigio, who loved GI Joe comic books and the X-men, couldn't get over the fact that I had flown in army helicopters during the war and had seen a city in ruins after a fierce battle. He couldn't get over the fact that the quiet man over there was a martial arts expert and a general who once commanded thousands.

"Yes and no," I told Remigio, trying to affect irony.

"What?"

"Well, yes because my people still suffer back home. No because I get to live in America."

"What's so great about America?" Remigio asked, trying to play the skeptic. He lived at the destination coveted by the world and, having friends who were immigrants, he felt the obligation to play down his privilege.

"Because in America you can grow up to be a movie star."
Remigio laughed.

The answer was blunt but to the point. I remember saying it loud, loud enough so that Father could hear it. But if he heard me, he, too busy absorbing the evening news, did not react.

In school the initial culture shock gave way to an easy assimilation. The shy boy who folded his arms and bowed his head when he asked permission to leave the house in Vietnam had become a quirky American kid whose hands were always in his jeans pockets and who mumbled in English "bye, Mom; bye, Dad" as he rushed to school, where he was popular.

My popularity was partly because I told family stories, wartime stories. Vietnam was the first television war and even children in America knew something, if only vaguely, about it. It gave me an entry to the American imagination that was otherwise unavailable to a kid from, say, Sri Lanka.

Did you see someone get killed?
Did your dad kill a lot of VCs?

In essence, I regurgitated stories my father told the family each evening, but I told them in English and told them well and in public, even as I was struggling to speak the language.

The blabbermouth aired family laundry for a place in the sun.

Did you know that my father met John Wayne in Vietnam and they talked about movies?

The first white person I met was when I was four and this actress name Jennifer Jones, you know, in Farewell to Arms, *visited Vietnam, and she held me in her arms while I wept. I was scared. I was like four years old.*

Yes, I saw lots of dead bodies. What's the big deal?
Yeah, I'm sure he killed a bunch of VCs!

My family was always surprised that, while the wounds of loss and defeat remained blistered and unhealed, I could talk about the past to strangers with such ease. I even made fun of what everyone considered sacred and unspeakable. But by speaking English and even telling crass boat people jokes and retelling Father's Vietnam War stories I was gaining some control over my tiny universe.

"Why are you telling family stories to your American friends?" my mother asked one night when I hung up the phone after talking with a classmate I was trying to impress. "Stop telling family secrets," she yelled. "Americans don't need to know anything about us."

"Yes, Mother," I said. But I couldn't.

"Stop speaking English in the house," my father ordered over dinner one night.

"Yes, Father," I answered in Vietnamese. But I couldn't do that either. Growing up in America, Vietnamese began to represent not just a language but a power play, one in which my role as the youngest son was absolute obedience, always inferior, always deferring to everyone else. Speaking English, on the other hand, became second nature to me. English loosened my tongue. "This is really unfair!" I would say aloud to my parents. Or, "But you're wrong! So wrong!" These phrases, spoken naturally by American children, are never spoken by Vietnamese counterparts in Vietnamese, and certainly not in Vietnam. My protests, though rare, it must be said, were always in English.

Secretly, I felt guilty. My parents shook their heads and sighed. I had, in their eyes, strayed. When my voice broke I naïvely believed that it had shattered, that somehow speaking English was the cause of my throaty voice, that I was being punished for speaking the language. But I was also fascinated with my own transformation. If my voice could change so radically, could the rest of me change also?

"Speak Vietnamese or don't speak at all," Father ordered.

"Yes, Father."

But instead I did the most awful thing I could do to him, to us. I fell silent.

Gradually the stories of my tropical country, the war stories told in English, grew strangely removed—like an antiseptic dream. I found that I had a sense of timing and could give a twist to the stories my father told to make them more interesting or dramatic. Sometimes I put myself in a war zone where I had never been. I became the map bearer. I even shot a machine gun from my father's helicopter in my retelling.

No, I never saw the irony, how much the past, glorious and bloody, still owned me. I only knew that by speaking up I was creating a self away from my family and, slowly, I was putting a frame around my history. By the time I was in high school the emotionality was drained from each new version, and the Vietnamese accent gave way to the Californian accent, and the longing for the lost homeland turned into self-mocking pathos, peppered with slang here, a wisecrack there. In telling the stories, in becoming extroverted, peculiar as it may sound, I felt as if I were slowly escaping my father's voice, my father's world, my father.

Liar. Where's the proof? Your father ain't no real general!
   Yeah, probably a corporal for all we know. Hahaha.
   He is so. I'll show you.
Here then is my second act of betrayal.

I was sixteen and full of bravado. I had a purple belt in karate, was practicing for brown. I got into fights. I hated being called a liar. I had to prove myself.

One afternoon I stole his uniform from his closet. In front of my friends I unfolded the uniform. We were partying in a garage a few blocks down the street, drinking beer, listening to music. Eyes widened. There were the oohs and ahhs.

I was nervous. There would be harsh consequences if Father found out. Of all the things we managed to bring with us from Vietnam, the uniform was the most sacred. Nevertheless I felt triumphant. All my stories were finally validated at that moment.

"Whoa, it's for real," Rick, my challenger, said, conceding. My friends took turns examining and marveling at the thing. It had been at the battlefields of Vietnam. It connected them to a world they saw on TV, a world they understood on some level or another that had somehow changed theirs. Many knew someone who went. A few even knew someone who didn't come back.

As they looked over the uniform, an idea hit me. I grabbed it and went to the bathroom and quickly changed into it. I came back out and started dancing. My friends laughed. A few shook their heads in disbelief. "Crazy kid," someone said.

Upon his words, an icy nausea rose in me and I stopped. I felt ridiculous. I felt I had crossed some invisible line and a part of me was offended by my own profanity. I staggered into the bathroom and checked myself. In the mirror Father's uniform hung loosely about me; I looked young and foolish in it. The uniform seemed to belong to somewhere else, in the dark, to memories, to mud and soil and burnt-out rice fields and bombed-out villages, and to the monsoon rain, to an unresolved war and all the profound sorrow and grief that I could neither fully subsume nor process. I felt like throwing up.

Then an unreasonable terror rose from the pit of my stomach, my heart pounding. I was afraid that I could not take it off. I felt entombed in a sea of khaki green fabric.

And it was then that I, retching, wanting to laugh at my own silliness but overwhelmed by guilt and a flood of tropical memories, plucked clumsily at the buttons, at my old skin, and wept.

Could a son ever redeem his father's lost war? What duty does an Americanized son owe his Vietnamese father in exile? What kind of territorial integrity could father and son hope to defend in America?

If, in the Vietnamese Confucian sense of things, there was no honor in retreat and escape from one's motherland, then why should a son honor his exiled father's political passion when the New World beckons?

I didn't know the answers to any of these questions. I didn't care to know them. I fled. To college. To own myself. To get away from the "we," the collective, from memories of blood and guts and napalm, away from the child who bowed to his dead ancestors and who sang the national anthem promising to give his last drop of blood to a homeland now lost.

To explore, to read and read and read, and to breathe, to experiment, to love, to immerse myself in the fantastic world of larger America, in carnal pleasure, in a place where Father cast no shadow.

During the cold war, a handful of Vietnamese in America who had advocated normalization with Vietnam were assassinated. One in particular I remember clearly because he was killed the same year that I began to write—began, that is, to really make a go at writing as a career and found, by a sheer stroke of luck, a part-time job as a journalist. The man was a writer and his name was Doan Van Toai. He was shot in San Francisco not too far from where I lived, shot for voicing his support of lifting the US trade embargo against Vietnam. Not only was there no condemnation of such a barbarous act within the community, there were murmurs of support for it, even among some of my relatives.

Political disagreement was dangerous in the community where rage and hatred against communism were so deep that, failing to get back at their perpetrators, many helplessly turned against themselves and their own. When someone dared speak within the community on issues relating to reconciliation with Vietnam during the cold war, there would be death threats and political denouncements. A person's standing in a community could easily be ruined, his business boycotted and protested if enough people believed that he was a leftist or a sympathizer of the Hanoi regime. Worse, he could, like Toai, be assassinated for his political point of view.

I was enraged. I did not agree with Toai. But I also couldn't help but see the obvious hypocrisy. A community that regularly waved its flags and banners in front of city halls across the United States to protest the Vietnamese communist regime for its atrocious human rights violations failed to be appalled at the murder of a Vietnamese American writer who was exercising a right that all of us had fled our homeland supposedly to safeguard.

The practice of silencing oppositions is typical of the old country, and it functions on a deep cultural level. Yet we were no longer living in the Old World. It had seemed to me that this blind expectation of obedience without serious dialogue—this assumption of basic shared values and shared political aspirations without serious and honest self-examination when we have become a minority in a country that expects public and civic participation in order to be heard, and in a global society where traditional values everywhere were being redefined and questioned—was, at best, politically and intellectually immature and, at worst, fertile ground for tyranny.

In the political context, simplified Confucian ideas are dangerous. Traditional views of patriotism, loyalty, filial piety, and respect, are reduced over the generations and are often inducted and transformed into forces that fuse ideological control over the masses. Communism, above all, had benefited greatly from this.

Democracy, on the other hand, can only flourish when opposite ideas are not only encouraged but respected. Father, who first taught me this idea, was as silent as the rest of the thinkers and intellectuals of the Vietnamese community on the subject of Toai's murder.

And so I pitted my skepticism against my father's nationalist passions and my parents' Confucian mores. I swapped my

Vietnamese name for an American—upon applying for US citizenship, I christened myself Andrew—and imagined a trajectory for myself radically different from that of the old man.

My parents had wanted me to be a doctor. I, who was pre-med at Berkeley, said no, having changed my mind. They offered me some money to work toward being a dentist. Again I said no. I have decided that I'm going to be a writer, I told them.

"What kind of writer?" Father asked, perplexed.

I didn't know exactly.

"Name a Vietnamese who is making a living as a writer in America," Father challenged.

There were, at the time, none.

"I will be one," I answered defiantly, fearing that if I weren't defiant enough my dream could be lost. Father, who on occasion jokingly referred to me as "his son, the Berkeley radical," cleared his throat and looked away disapprovingly. My mother blamed the "craziness" of Berkeley. My older brother, who had returned to his dutiful role as the eldest son in the family and become an engineer, called me a hippie.

It occurred to me then that for children of Asian immigrants who covet an expressive, creative life, there is often a hidden price more costly than the regular fares—poverty, years of drudging in the dark, self-doubt, and so on—and it is one that wafts with the faint odor of dishonor. In the eyes of those who had brought him to the new shore, who struggled to send him to a university, and who strapped their hopes and dreams upon his back, he has committed an act of betrayal, giving up the immigrants' sense of pragmatism for the fanciful—a selfish, ungracious act.

If he is to strive into the wilderness called the world of arts and literature, then he is to strive alone, making his own map, carving his own path. There, where few of his kind have ventured, he must now build for himself a new home, all the while his family, his clan back in the village, shake their heads and sigh, waiting for him to fail.

But so be it. I played the skeptic, the radical.

I kept my distance.

Many years passed...

My father is a conservative. I'm a liberal. He's a nationalist and I'm a globalist. He's a very good tennis player and, in retirement, still plays. I am terrible at tennis, at sports in general, and rarely play. He still practices martial arts, while I long ago gave up karate, opting now for the gentler form of yoga. He votes regularly as clockwork and has been consistently Republican ever since he obtained his US citizenship. When I do vote, it's for the Democrats or even the Greens.

He supported the US invasion of Iraq. I was adamantly against it and marched in protest on the streets of San Francisco among hundreds of thousands of protesters. He sees the world in term of geopolitics, top down, and I, a bit like my mother, absorb it first through the heart before trying to make sense of it with the head. He likes to talk politics, but when challenged he often turns gloomy, and when challenged with passion he says, "Forget it!" Once while I was visiting, he lost his temper and said in Vietnamese, "Shut up! I don't like it when you speak only English in the house." And that, as they say, was the end of that.

His love for his homeland keeps him in many ways immune to the seduction of America, of expansive California, but I have long ago taken glimpses of the Golden State, its marvelous possibilities, its promises of the self fully realized, and learned to bask in its cosmopolitan sheen.

Vietnam remains his only true interest. My interests lie elsewhere. His compass points steadfastly, unwavering, toward Southeast Asia. Mine spins and points at several directions on any given day. He is against normalization with Vietnam, against trade with Vietnam, against travels to Vietnam. He is, conversely, deeply in love with Vietnam, with the idea of a communist-free Vietnam. Anyone who goes there is, therefore, a traitor to the cause. When normalization happened under a democratic president, who later traveled to Vietnam, he became quite ill. And each time he hears of others of his generation, those of the old ruling class—ex-military officials, ex-congressmen, and so on—who have gone back to visit since the end of the cold war, he would shake his head and mutter French curses— *"Contes!" "Cochons!" "Putain!" "Merde!"*—under his breath.

When I went back for the first time, he thought it was a big mistake. I went anyway. Traveling the length of Vietnam by train for the first time, I had at times wondered if Father was, back in San Jose, throwing French curses at me. Now each time I go, he doesn't say anything at all.

I was against normalization, but after I visited Vietnam I changed my mind and supported it. Yes, I wanted to see a free Vietnam and had declared that I will pop open a bottle of Roederer Cristal when the country adopts a multiparty system and allows freedom of expression to exist, and I wrote articles saying normalization was a step in the right direction. Interaction spurs change, I reasoned. He thinks I'm politically immature and wishy-washy. I think he is, like many of his generation, mired in the cold war and inflexible. I think he does not understand what motivates real people and, while astute in the way nations clash against each other politically, holds oddly little insight into the workings of the human heart.

Father will not go back. The exile general won't allow himself that luxury. His stance against his enemies is resolute, even if most of those who fought against him are dead or in retirement. Vietnam—the crucible, the source—for him is an impossible distance to travel.

Vietnam for me has been for a while now one of many possible destinations. But it's also an enigma. I can and cannot go home again. If the past still owns me, the country, now readily accessible and familiar, does not.

Yet Father, a student of history, does not expect it to be kind. He understands the way tragedy strikes—which is to say cruelly and with regularity against the best and the brightest—and that, as he once observed, human sufferings have their intrinsic grandeur, and he is, therefore, not entirely an unhappy man.

Whereas I...

So are you sad you lost the war?

There were times, dear Remigio, when I was very envious of you. History happened to others on TV and you—you who grew up where everyone else wanted to live—could always change the channel. Other times I felt sorry for you. Your immunity from history robs you of the awe and appreciation of seeing how its powerful flow and surge can change everyone, near or far. Unappreciative of your own history, you are deprived of the marvels of the history of others. In the center of the empire, the happenings of the world seemed to have barely touched you at all.

Yet your question after all these years still leaves me breath-less. Decades have passed since helicopters carried refugees away from the American embassy's rooftop and communist tanks rolled through the city where I once lived, and still I find myself some gray morning, quite unexpectedly, struggling to rise above the sadness.

Transnationalism, multiculturalism, citizens of the world—these speak of a bright and enlightened age of a post–cold war era, a world of freedom and openness, one that I latch onto so readily in contrast to what had been previously my predicament: exile, refugee, minority, South Vietnamese, war's loser. Sometimes it feels as if the world of the multilingual, sophisticated cosmopolitan is but a salve, a compensation to the unhealed wounds of exile, a veil over immense losses.

It has taken me a long time to come to the realization that for those whose lives have been inordinately altered by forces of history, the personal is to the historical the way brooks and rivers are to the sea. James Baldwin's riddle is rhetorical, after all, when he asks in one piercing essay, "Which of us has overcome his past?" and promptly answers in another, "People are trapped in history and history is trapped in them."

Take love for example. When I began to write, it was not about the war or its aftermath. I wrote about my own broken heart. I tried to capture what it was like to lose someone who had been my preoccupation throughout my college life, who was then, in fact, my life. I was too close to the subject, as it turned out. Too hurt to do the story justice. But the raw emotions unearthed another set of older memories simmering underneath. To lose someone you loved dearly, someone with whom you created an intimate world, with whom you shared a private language and a routine, is to be exiled. Yet I have been exiled before. The brokenhearted adult found himself reexperiencing the emotions of the brokenhearted child who stood alone on the beach of Guam, missing his classmates, his dogs, fretting about his father, wondering if he'd ever see his homeland again.

I wrote some more. My sadness opened a trapdoor to the past. Memories came gushing up, made themselves clear once more. A child forced to flee. The long line for food under a punishing sun in a green city made of army tents. People weeping themselves to sleep. The altar where faded photographs of the dead stared out

forlornly, the incense still burning but the living gone. I yearned
for my memories.

I wrote some more.

I began to go back.

If one cannot escape one's history one ought to embrace it fully,
dear Remigio. But by embrace I do not mean to dwell in the losses
or to live in the constant state of mourning or, worse still, to be
bound by lost glories. The more mature response to one's tragedy
is not hatred nor resentment but spiritual resilience with which one
can, again and again, struggle to transcend one's own biographical
limitations. History is trapped in me, indeed, but history is also
mine to work out, to disseminate, to discern and appropriate, and
to finally transform into aesthetic self-expression.

To put it another way, one can, with due respect, chase Baldwin's
grim discernment with N. Scott Momaday's astute council: "Anything
is bearable as long as you can make a story out of it."

Mine then is a battle I suspect many children of immigrants and
refugees, whose biographies are borne from incongruous histories,
are waging now across America, across, for that matter, the globe.
It is one that took root in the cold war but found its power in the
aftermath—borne, that is, of the clash and, therefore, inevitably,
the marvelous marriages of civilizations. We are growing up in a
world that is being redefined by the various forces of globalization:
unprecedented mass movements and porous borders and high-
tech gadgetries and cultural exchanges.

Our struggles, in many ways, are more contemporary than
and as challenging as the older generations' continual clamor for
a regime change in another nation across the ocean. It is a war of
many fronts. There is that treacherous space between the traditional "We" and the ambitious American "I" where we had to navigate.
Then there is that struggle against the constant thread of discrimi-
nation and racism. There is, more importantly, the constant search
to define and redefine ourselves in a pluralistic, global society that
remains at best ignorant and at worst hostile to our presence, our
histories, our biographies, our stories.

So yes, sad, but also hopeful.

The America that received my family and me in the mid-seventies was an America that could not possibly have fathomed the coming of a Pacific Century. The rise of the Far East, its cultural and economic influences lapping now at the American shores, seem to have taken everyone by surprise. Like sidewalk vendors hawking bitter melons and bok choy and lemongrass on the streets here in San Francisco, private passions, too, are spilling out with candor into the public place. Indian writers becoming American men and women of letters. Sushi being sold in high school cafeterias. HMOs now offering acupuncture. And feng shui becoming a household word.

Ours is fast becoming a postmodern world where traditions not only coexist but often commingle. Thus does the self, open to change, become a multitude, constantly being constructed, constantly adding homelands. In such a world there is enormous confusion, but its ground is also inordinately fertile for the imagination.

From that point of view, the Confucian idea I like best is the one that's practiced least. It assumes everyone is a human being in the making, not cookie molded; that, with resilience and determination, there is a better person to be forged from experience. Confucian scholar and Harvard professor Tu Weiming once said in an interview, "I am determined to transform the conditioning forces originally constraining me to be a limited human being— my ethnicity, my gender, my socialization, and so forth—into a concrete manifestation of myself as the center of relationships."

And so am I.

These days I tell my stories with a different intent than when I was a refugee boy during junior high school recess. No longer wanting to bury my past, I write with a stubborn, binding conviction in my heart that my story, too—fragmented as it is and spanning the Ocean Pacific—is an American experience.

But the war to assert oneself, one's history, need not be a war. The man who sees the world with its many dimensions simultaneously is, in many ways, a blessed man. To be defined by incongruous histories is not necessarily an impediment these days, and from the point of view of someone in transition, dancing at the far end of a continuum, they are the stuff from which one builds bridges to otherwise disconnected, seemingly opposed ideas and once far-flung spheres. They take their reference points across borders, languages, time zones, and often from two or three different continents. Transnationalism, a world complicated by memories and ambitions and multiple connections, once a peculiar space, is now a condition shared by much of humanity. Its unique and rounded characters refute simplification.

I see now with clarity my writing life. It has come to rest within me the task of marrying two otherwise dissimilar and, often, conflicting narratives. Vietnam and America are vying for my soul. But between Vietnam and America, for me, too, is an undiscovered country, and it is an epic in the making.

I came home to my parents for a visit on the eve of another war. On TV the US Army was moving forward to Baghdad. Sorties emblazoned the Arabian nights. Father in his white *gi* with a black belt was on his way out to the backyard to practice his martial arts but stopped and watched.

His face was grim and pensive. I watched him. The ice was melting in my whiskey glass. The alcohol gave me courage. "Father, are you still angry that you lost the war?"

If he was surprised by my question he didn't show it. He looked out the sliding door where the swimming pool shone bright and blue. Once a very handsome man, the Black Panther of the South had turned thin and gray in America. Although his back remained military straight and that solitary air still defined and owned him, there were age spots on his skin and deep wrinkles had set in around his eyes, which seemed to me infinitely sad.

"Of course, I'm still angry, and sad," he said. "We were abandoned by the US. So many of my friends sacrificed for nothing and Vietnam is ruled by a repressive regime."

"Why didn't you stay and fight?"

Father sighed and started to tighten the belt around his waist. The dying sun was on his face. He squinted. "After hearing the message of surrender on the radio, I decided I had to leave."

I was glad I'd been drinking when I asked the next question. "Did you consider *tu thu*? Did you think of suicide also, like the other generals?"

He took his time. On TV, a CNN reporter was talking about troop movements. Father's attention was divided. "The generals who committed suicide were corps and division commanders whose units were still combat effective. They committed suicide because they didn't want to surrender their units to the enemy. The reality was that by choosing to die these generals upheld the highest level of the Confucian concept of honor."

"But you didn't," I pressed on. I meant to say more than that. I wanted to say that he didn't uphold that ultimate concept himself. I also wanted to say that I am so glad that he didn't. That his un-Confucian act, as it were, had resulted in an American life for himself, for his family, and it had meant for his children trips to Disneyland and Europe and Mexico, a semblance of normalcy.

I'm glad my father did not honor the Confucian ideals enough to die for them. I'm glad that love moved him as much as duty and honor did. I think suicide to honor one's commitment to a cause is overrated. I think wanting to live to honor life itself—no matter how wretched, even at the cost of humiliation and loss of honor—takes a greater kind of courage.

But the language of intimacy and love in the Vietnamese household is subterraneous and rarely ever spoken. In Vietnamese families, phrases like "I love you," "I'm proud of you," "I forgive you," are virtually nonexistent. So I, the writer who gave lectures and speeches at universities, lost courage at home, took a sip of my drink, and said nothing.

Father looked at me. "This was a question of choice. I didn't commit suicide because I was not a unit commander at that moment and because President Thieu should be held responsible for our defeat, not the unit commanders in the field."

On the other hand, the inept president had inadvertently spared my father from the fate that befell his comrades in arms by arresting him and, thereby, removing him from his soldiers. If Thieu had been an artful strategist, the war would have gone on longer, and my father and many others would be long dead. I hadn't felt thankful to the man before, but at that moment I was.

Still, Father's choice to leave at the end of the war came with a price—the sting of defeat, the stigma of dishonor. I could hear it all in his voice, which was sad and soft. "I bear the loss of the homeland," he said as he looked out to the reflecting water of the pool, "but I know the Marxist system will eventually collapse. When that happens I hope I'll still be around. I'll have the opportunity to go back to a free Vietnam."

With that the conversation ended. He went outside. In his white martial arts uniform, Father started to kick and block and chop.

I turned off the TV, turned off another war, and watched him instead. And as I watched, a memory made itself clear. I was still in high school. One day I looked into my father's wallet for some money and found a picture of myself: four years old and standing in front of a pile of donated fabric and clothes from the United States to be distributed by my mother to flood victims in the Mekong Delta. It was the only picture he kept in his wallet near the end of the war, and it was the only picture he brought with him to the United States when he boarded the naval ship that took him out of his homeland. If I was merely surprised when I first found the picture, the memory of that discovery and the faint nausea of the liquor caused me to close my eyes as a deep pang of regret rose in me.

As far as Confucian ethics between fathers and sons are concerned, I think the idea that should be promoted is one where the relationship is defined in terms of love and affection and even obeisance. The idea to be demoded is the one based on the rigid demands of power, of authorities and uncritical obedience.

Yet even by my own definition, by my own standards, by what I strive toward in adulthood, I have not been a good son. Ours has been a cold if polite relationship since I left home. When I visit, I still fall into habit, into the old ways, which are difficult, oblique, and inarticulate. I still play a mute child at my parents' home. I fail to fill the growing gap between us. Behind my silence, my polite demeanor, I grieve.

Out on the courtyard my father danced his martial arts dance. Against the orange Californian sky at twilight the exile-general seemed a lone figure against the last light.

"Arrggh! Arrggh! Arrggh!" he shouted as he moved—fists punching the air, legs sweeping invisible enemies—oblivious to the snickering neighbors and the fleeing sparrows. He is forever prepared for that last trip home, nourished by his vision of glorious repatriation, if only to dance one last dance on his enemy's grave.

* * *

That old dream again…

Sometimes I'm a bird. Other times I'm fully human. Always it's a dive into the clear blue ocean. Bird, fish, me as a child, me as an adult—no matter—in the dream we all go straight to the bottom. We try to excavate. Retrieve something hard to see. With bloody fingers. With torn bill. With bruised lips.

A rusted gun. In the dream the gun turns into a vague object, or a sorry-looking rock, or it changes its shape continuously and loses texture. This morning it simply dissolves into sand, into mud, and sifts through my clutching fingers.

I wake. Restless at dawn.

I take to strolling aimlessly throughout my parents' house.

I open drawers. I look into family albums. I search the faces of the dead on the family altar.

What am I looking for?

I don't know exactly but, absentmindedly, I keep searching.

I open the family closet in the hallway. I stand and stare into the darkness until something in the back, hidden behind a row of business suits and coats and sweaters, catches my eyes, my attention. Alone on a hook, it's an enshrouded shadow wrapped in a wrinkled plastic cover.

I reach in and take it out. I place it on the dining table and study it. On each lapel are three stars, meticulously sewn, and above his name there's that symbol of a fist with three dots signifying his martial arts degree. In its right breast pocket is a talisman given to him by one of his loyal soldiers to keep him from harm. Father kept it throughout the war and through the years in America. The khaki fabric itself has aged and feels, through the thin plastic membrane, strangely soft to the touch.

Upstairs my parents stir awake. I hear footsteps and water running. Light seeps through the window. Mother's little garden beside the pool, with its jasmine and rosebushes, now pulses with birdsongs.

Almost time to go, the weekend visit nears ending. A kiss then for my father before leaving: I tear a hole through the army uniform's plastic cover, lean close, and sniff. Sniff again. There is no odor now of gunpowder, no smell of scorched earth, no cigar stench—only the faint smell of camphor, old dust.

Love, Money, Prison, Sin, Revenge

March 1994

On the afternoon of April 4, 1991, fifteen years, one month, and twenty-six days after the end of the Vietnam War, four Vietnamese youths armed with semiautomatic pistols stormed into a Good Guys electronics store on Stockton Boulevard in Sacramento and held forty-one people hostage. Speaking heavily accented and broken English, they issued what the *Sacramento Bee* described as "a series of bizarre demands." They wanted a helicopter to fly to Thailand and fight the Viet Cong, $4 million, four bulletproof vests, and forty pieces of one-thousand-year-old ginseng root.

While a crowd gathered across the street (some enthusiasts equipped with their own camcorders), TV reporters informed viewers that three of the gunmen were brothers—Loi Khac Nguyen, 21; Pham Khac Nguyen, 19; and Long Khac Nguyen, 17—and the last, Cuong Tran, 16, was Long Nguyen's best friend. The Nguyen brothers had come from a poor Vietnamese Catholic family headed by an ex-sergeant of the South Vietnamese Army. All four were altar boys. Three of the youths had dropped out of school or had been expelled. None had been able to find a steady job.

The gunmen could be seen on live television behind the store's glass doors, strolling back and forth with their firearms, their hostages bound at their feet. Sacramento County Sheriff Glen Craig, who had implanted listening devices in the store, reported that the gunmen were jubilant at seeing themselves and hearing their names on TV—"Oh, ah, we're going to be movie stars!" The sheriff had also told reporters that the gunmen belonged to a

51

loose-knit gang called the Oriental Boys—an error, as it turned out, since police couldn't prove their membership in any gang.

As the siege wore on, negotiations between the gunmen and the taut-faced, gray-haired sheriff reached a stalemate. The gunmen, for their part, had grown increasingly edgy and refused to negotiate after authorities met only part of one demand—providing them with a single bulletproof jacket. Sheriff Craig, on the other hand, later told reporters that the four would not "focus on any single demand. They were attempting to gain notoriety, attention, and, perhaps, some transportation out of the country."

Eight and a half hours later, after the gunmen had wounded two of the hostages, a SWAT team raided the store on live television. Three of the young men were killed immediately, but not before one of them sprayed the hostages with bullets, killing two employees—John Lee Fritz and Kris Sohne—and a customer—Fernando Gutierrez—and wounding eight more. Loi Nguyen, the oldest, and the one who wore the bulletproof jacket, was seriously wounded. He was tried on forty-nine felony counts and three counts of murder. He plead not guilty.

As I watched this tragedy unfold on my TV set that night, I remember being overwhelmed by an irrational fear. It was the fear that the Vietnam War had somehow been renewed by those gunmen and by those helicopters hovering over the store. And although I was on the safe side of the screen now and judging their barbaric acts, I was not without this singular sense of foreboding: six years ago I could have been one of them.

If the story of the Good Guys ended in carnage on the linoleum floor of an electronics store, it began an ocean and an epic journey away, nourished by numerous subterranean streams. It is in those streams that I am foundering. I am at once too close and too far from their story. Though an American journalist now, I came to this country as a Vietnamese refugee, the son of an army officer. The young men and I are children of defeated warriors. In their demands I hear the thematic echo of vengeance, that forms and shapes many Vietnamese youths who grow up in America. Perhaps all of this binds me to the Good Guys hostage-takers nearly two decades after the last US helicopter hovered over a burning Saigon before heading toward the South China Sea.

When I asked for directions, the blond kid on Stockton Boulevard rattled off names of generic American landmarks in an amiable tone: Midas...Shakey's Pizza...Carl's Jr....Man, you can't miss it. Turn left at the House of Fabrics. Next to it you'll see the Good Guys.

Inside, the first thing you notice is yourself. Walk through the glass door and a dozen camcorders give you back your reflections on the various TV sets. For as little as $549, you could be (oh, ah) your own movie star.

I saw but tried not to look at my own faces on those TV screens. The faces—my faces—appeared expressionless, the thick brows slightly raised, touched perhaps by a tinge of skepticism. I do not believe in instant fame, had always thought Andy Warhol's prediction an odd American curse.

But teenagers are daily worshipers in this secular temple of high-tech consumerism, their eyes mesmerized by the *son et lumière*. At the Nintendo counter, five Asian teens vied to compete in the world championships of Street Fighter II. At the cellular phone display two Latino girls pretended to gossip using those palm-sized communicators. And at the store's far end, a hundred or so TV sets formed a kind of electronic wall that talked and sang and showed the shopper the panorama of America—talk shows, soap operas, commercials. A fat housewife described her sex life on a dozen or so screens. In a hushed tone, she related intimate details of her marital betrayal to Oprah and fourteen million other people—"I never told anybody this but..."—and managed to blush.

It is here, in this postmodern American public square, that the ethnic private meets the mainstream public. At dinnertime on the night of the Good Guys siege, Papa and Mama Nguyen suddenly saw their three eldest boys holding American hostages at the neighborhood electronics store. One can assume that their sons were simultaneously watching their own drama on dozens of TV sets. It is a kind of instantaneous real-life opera made popular by television these days, the blood opera with all nuances flattened so viewers get only a reporter's sound bites and vivid endings. Narrative is shaved to the bone, history and background ignored.

That sort of ignorance is peculiarly American, or so it seems to many of the twelve thousand Vietnamese in the Sacramento area. A few who watched the siege recall a dangerous combination of arrogance and confusion among the TV reporters and especially the authorities. "They ran around like chickens without heads," said one Vietnamese man who volunteered to help the police but was turned away. "The boys were Vietnamese Catholics and the sheriff initially had a Laotian monk at the scene," he said.

Yet clues that would have helped the sheriff and the journalists unlock the gunmen's psyches were just minutes from the Good Guys, in Little Saigon. In a mini-mall a mile or so away a video store called Ngoc Thao (Precious Herb) catered to a Vietnamese clientele. Colorful posters of gangsters and cops holding Uzis and of ancient swordsmen in silk brocades flying above temple rooftops covered the walls and windows. Here, as in many other video stores frequented by local Vietnamese in Sacramento, one can find one-thousand-year-old ginseng roots—the precious cure-all usually discovered by the lucky hero in kung fu epics—as well as other magical panaceas and cursed swords. They're in the hundreds of Hong Kong videos, dubbed in Vietnamese, that line the shelves.

The cashier of the video store, a heavily made-up woman, was having a busy day. Like a high priestess with holy water, she dispensed pieces of Asia's fabled past to hordes of homesick Vietnamese.

"Sister, when is the *Royal Tramp* video coming out? I've been waiting for months."

"Sister, we want *Dragon Palms* and *The Revenge of Black Orchid*. I hear the woman in *Orchid* is the best fighter and, like a man, kills everyone who assassinated her parents."

"Aunty, how much does a karaoke machine cost? Everybody in my family is dying to be a rock 'n' roll star."

At the entrance, an eight-year-old holding a plastic bag filled with kung fu videos was his old man's pride and joy. Papa urged

Youngest Son to say something to a friend, an army buddy wearing a fatigue jacket. Youngest Son shrugged, then, without enthusiasm, recited a quote from a movie: "Honorable Father, I must leave you now and find a mentor to learn the martial art way. I will avenge our family honor after I have mastered the Iron Palms of Death."

The two men laughed and applauded the mythological voice of China, a voice that provides a kind of parochial snare in the Americanization process. Thanks to CNN, satellite dishes, cable TV, VCRs, jumbo jets, camcorders, and fax machines, integration turns retro-future-active: technology renews old myths, shrinks oceans, packages memories, melts borders, rejuvenates old passions, redefines the assimilation process. For Asian children immigrating to America today, their parents' homelands are no longer as far away as they were for children in earlier times. The American-born Vietnamese boy who mouths ancient wisdoms may not know their meaning, may never, for that matter, master the Iron Palms of Death, but somehow Asia has already exuded mysticism into his soul. Indeed, the alluring incense, the singsong languages, the communal and familial Confucian values of loyalty and obligation, the Old World gestures of self-sacrifice and revenge—all that earlier generations of American-born Asians tried so hard to exorcise—is now in style, evidenced in the Little Saigons and Little Seouls that dot so many California urban landscapes.

Two days after the Good Guys siege, a *Sacramento Bee* photo that ran the length of the page showed the Nguyen brothers' parents standing in their living room as if facing a firing squad. Though stricken with grief, Bim Khac and Sao Thi Nguyen admitted journalists into their tiny two-bedroom unit in the Laura Dawn Manor Apartments, a two-story structure rented out mostly to Southeast Asian families.

The photo shows a sagging sofa, a VCR, and, of course, a large TV set. On top of the TV stands a South Vietnamese flag—three red horizontal stripes against a gold background—representing a country that no longer exists. On the opposite wall, a three-tier shrine displays crucifixes, statues of Mary, Joseph, and Jesus and various martyred saints, all with mournful faces.

The Nguyens and their six children spent four months in a refugee camp in Indonesia before coming to the United States in the early 1980s. In Sacramento they were receiving Aid to Families with Dependent Children. The ex-sergeant from the South Vietnamese Army, who is active in church, said through an interpreter that he was no help to his children when it came to explaining American things such as homework or the news on TV. Still, wasn't what he wanted for his children the same as what any Vietnamese parent wants—that they do well in school but keep "Vietnamese traditions"?

"Please tell the people of Sacramento I am very sorry for what my sons have done," the patriarch offered. Asked how his quiet, obedient boys wound up becoming hostage-takers, Nguyen and his wife provided only a miserable silence.

This is the silence of an older generation of Vietnamese refugees who no longer feel anchored anywhere but in their impoverished homes. The exterior landscape belongs to America, strange and nonsensical, not their true home. Inside, many Vietnamese refugees tend to raise their children with stern rules—the way they themselves were raised back home. Vietnamese is spoken, with familial personal pronouns—Youngest Son, Older Sister, Aunt, Father, Great Uncle, and so on—lacing every sentence to remind the speakers and the listeners of their status in the Confucian hierarchical scheme of things. These parents are unprepared for children who lead dual lives, who may in fact commit rash and incomprehensibly violent acts—not at all the docile and obedient Vietnamese children they had hoped to raise.

"They are no longer really Vietnamese, nor are they really Americans," said a former teacher—who recently came from Vietnam and now lives on welfare in Sacramento—of his own children. He called their tangled assimilation "crippled Americanization."

For Loi, Pham, and Long Nguyen and Cuong Tran, who failed school and grew up between the Good Guys electronics store and the Ngoc Thao, there existed two separate notions: notoriety and revenge, revenge being the stronger impulse. One encourages public displays (i.e., confessing on *Oprah*, or holding shoppers hostage and giving incoherent speeches) that may lead mainstream

America to acknowledge that they exist. The other fulfills the old man's extraterritorial passion—"helicopters to Thailand to kill Viet Cong"—and rejects America as the wasteland.

To grow up Vietnamese in America, after all, is to grow up with the legacy of belonging to the loser's side and to endure all that entails. To grow up in America is to desire individual fame and glory, a larger sense of the self. Driving on Stockton Boulevard, it suddenly occurs to me that, while I myself might have learned to walk that strange Vietnamese-American hyphen, it continues to hurl other young and hapless Vietnamese down into a dark and bottomless pit.

After Good Guys, the media offered a variety of explanations. One had to do with the chronology of waves, as in waves of Vietnamese immigrants. The first wave of refugees who came to America in 1975, my wave, comprised intellectuals, educators, army officers, skilled civil servants, professionals—Vietnam's best and brightest, those who had not experienced Vietnam under communist rule. This wave adjusted relatively well to American life, to an America of the 1970s that was economically stable and motivated, in part by guilt, to be generous to the newly arrived: there were English as a Second Language teachers, low-interest loans, job-training programs.

The later wave, the boat people who came in the eighties, were a different group—people who had been traumatized by reeducation camps, cannibalism, rape, robbery, drownings at the hands of sea pirates, people who had suffered a chaotic and broken society back home under communist hands. These less-skilled, less-educated refugees were ill equipped to adjust to a less-generous America.

But there were deeper currents that fed this particular second-wave refugee family that the media failed to detect. According to one Vietnamese social worker who knew the Nguyen family well, the parents had been burned not once but twice by communism. They fled to the South in 1954 when Catholics were persecuted by Ho Chi Minh and his army, and then they fled Saigon as boat people a few years after the communists ransacked the South in 1975. Communist crimes, Viet Cong crimes, human-rights abuses by the

Hanoi regime—all are meticulously documented by Vietnamese Catholic newspapers and magazines in the United States. The Viet Cong, whom the eldest Nguyen boy barely remembered, nevertheless figured as the prime villains in the household cosmology: they were the chief cause of their family's suffering in America, the robbers of their father's dignity, the blasphemers of the crucifix in their church called the Vietnamese Catholic Martyrs.

The Nguyen brothers and Cuong Tran (whose more-affluent Chinese Vietnamese parents, unlike the Nguyens, refused to open their doors to journalists) were reportedly Hong Kong movie fanatics. All four youths watched the highly stylized films whose sword-crossing heroes and gun-toting detectives and gangsters duked it out amid Hong Kong high-rises, filling their waking dreams with homilies to honor, fraternal loyalty, betrayal, and revenge.

To many Vietnamese living in Sacramento, these Hong Kong videos are the real culprit in the Good Guys shootout. Gangster films like John Woo's *A Better Tomorrow* and *Bullet in the Head* were the rage among Vietnamese youth in the late 1980s. It was in reenacting these gang shooting scenes, some speculate, that the gunmen coolly flipped coins to decide which of the hostages would take the first bullet.

In *Bullet in the Head,* three best friends—blood brothers from Hong Kong looking to make a name for themselves (they had been losers up to that point)—travel to Vietnam during the war to smuggle illegal ampicillin. With the help of an assassin, they end up fighting everyone, including the Viet Cong. Though profit is their original quest, they are also searching for their lost souls; they cannot decide whether they are good guys or bad guys. Along the way, the brothers are captured by the Viet Cong and tortured. They escape when Army of the Republic of Vietnam helicopters arrive and attack the Viet Cong stronghold.

What moves the plot along and prompts young Vietnamese viewers to whooping-oohing cheers is the escalating interplay of terror and death from one scene to the next, culminating in a betrayal of camaraderie and leading to vengeance.

A few weeks after Good Guys, Sacramento police received a mysterious letter signed by the Brothers of the Dragon: "On 4-4-91 you have killed our brothers in Sacramento for no reason," it announced. "For this reason there must be revenge. The Brothers of the Dragon have decided in a meeting a lesson will be made." On the margins of the letter were the Vietnamese words that embody the Hong Kong movie gangster mythos, words that many Vietnamese gang members have tattooed on their own skin: *Tinh, Tien, Tu, Toi, Thu*—Love, Money, Prison, Sin, Revenge.

I try but cannot reach Loi Nguyen. His defense lawyer, Linda M. Parisi, refuses to answer my letters and phone calls. She traveled to Vietnam at her own expense to better understand the case and is known to be extremely protective of her clients.

Then I go to interview his parents, both under psychiatric care. Although I imagine myself to be an American journalist, the closer I come to their home the more I realize this has been a false assumption. Sitting in my car outside the Laura Dawn Manor, I am overwhelmed by fear and guilt. Once the door opens and the old couple welcomes me in, in my mother's language, I know I will lose all perspective. An American journalist would ask the old couple, "How do you feel?" but I can't. Among Vietnamese, a collective understanding assumes that we have all suffered an epic loss, so it is pointless to ask. Once inside I might as well put away the notepad and declare my loyalty to the old couple, whatever their shortcomings.

I am also aware that I will somehow benefit from their tragedy. Whereas the youths were inarticulate and failed to become stars, I, the one who has a public voice, am about to gain a measure of notoriety as the teller of their sensational tale. Irrational as it may be, I feel like a cannibal. And this, perhaps more than any other reason, is why I can't bring myself to knock on their door.

Defeated, I return to San Francisco, the city of glassy high-rises and rolling hills, where I live. It is, I realize, a different narrative that I am after now, one that moves from the incidental toward the historical. I go to Tu Lan, a Vietnamese coffee shop in the Tenderloin District where Vietnamese men wearing unkempt army jackets argue about Vietnamese politics in low voices on a weekday afternoon. Cigarette smoke hangs in the air like a white mosquito net. A song entitled "Mother Vietnam: We Are Still Here" echoes from the stereo.

Thuan, a twenty-two-year-old who came to the United States five years ago, stares at my laptop with large, sad eyes as I jot down some notes. Of course he has heard about the Good Guys siege, which has become a legend among his friends.

"What those guys tried to do is to make America notice us. To me they're martyrs. Brother, America doesn't care if we live or die. At night I see Vietnamese kids wandering the streets like ghosts. Some run away from home, some have no home to go to. Some travel from one city to the next looking for something, not knowing what. Maybe if I had come early and become articulate and educated like you, it would be different. But it's too late. Now I'm just a nobody. No education. I'm just stupid like a pig."

Thuan, whose father died in a communist reeducation camp, has an easy explanation for the hostage-takers' demands. "The ginseng roots are to increase your internal strength tenfold. Everybody knows that. Some say you can see in the dark if you drink enough tea made from it. The older the roots are, the more potent and powerful. The helicopters are for revenge. If I were the sheriff, Brother, I'd have given them the helicopter and ammunition and sent them to Vietnam to kill all the fucking Viet Cong in the world."

If I were articulate and educated like you, Brother...

But no matter how articulate a Vietnamese becomes, dear Brother, when we set foot on the American shore, history is already against us. Vietnam goes on without us; America goes on without acknowledging us. We, like our defeated fathers, have become beside the point, a footnote in a small chapter of the history book. Our mythology is merely a private dream in America: there is no war to fight, no heroic quest, no territory to defend, no visible enemies.

I remember that day when my father remained behind in Vietnam while my family and I escaped to Guam. I remember sitting on a beach near our refugee camp with a hundred or so Vietnamese countrymen, listening to the British Broadcasting Corporation detail Saigon's fall. I heard screams, saw wailing women tear their hair, saw men beat the sand with their fists, saw children weep. Then as the sun set, an old man stood up and sang our national anthem: "Let's go to the battlefields together, why

regret one's life? National blood debts must be avenged by blood....
O, citizens, sacrifice your lives for the flag..."

And so on. But no one joined the old man in the song. There
was only silence. Then my mother whispered a challenge: "We are
no longer citizens, we are now *ma troi* (wandering ghosts)." And
the sun, blood red, dissolved into the horizon where Vietnam was,
behind my mother's words.

Silence enshrouded the two-bedroom apartment in San
Francisco where ten of us—two grandmothers, six grandchildren,
two struggling sisters—made our new home. My body hurtled
through the narrow, dark corridors like a bat, avoiding the tiny
kitchen where only the women were allowed entrance (and from
which the smell of fish sauce seeped out). We ate in silence (but
always with the television turned on) in the dining room that
served as another bedroom at night. We waited silently in line for
the bathroom, took showers together, slept together, yet we negoti-
ated these intimate acts with the gestures of mimes. Why talk at all
if everything to be voiced would only invoke sorrow? Where once
we had been lively upper-middle-class families in that tropical
country so far away, here we were mousy, impoverished, miserable
exiles living in a deep, dark hole.

The Vietnamese refugee's first self-assessment in America is,
inevitably, of his own helplessness. It is characterized by blushing,
by looking down at one's feet, by avoiding eye contact, and by waiting: for welfare and food stamps, for the free clinic exam, for jackets donated by charity, for green cards. As for the Vietnamese child,
at some point he comes to the brutal realization that "his" side has
lost and "his" nation is gone; that his parents are inarticulate fools
in a new country called America, and he must face the outside
world alone.

As I did. One autumn morning in the locker room of my junior
high, Johnny M., the blond and blue-eyed boy standing gloriously
naked, asked, "Refugee boy, which side were you on? The winner's
or the loser's?"

English still an unbendable language on my tongue, I answered,
"Me: loser's side!" The locker room immediately erupted into a

chorus of laughter, and I felt Johnny's wet towel on my face—the white flag, I supposed, to surrender with.

In geography class, Mrs. Collier brought out the new map of East Asia. Vietnam, that country coiling in the voluptuous shape of an S, was no longer mine. It was repainted now in a uniform color—red—the South flooded with blood. Mrs. Collier didn't know why, exactly, that strange Asian kid, so quiet, suddenly buried his face in his arms and wept.

It was my father's passion that I was feeling. A couple of months after our arrival, my father, the defeated general, made it to America. He and Aunty Tuyet's husband, a paratroop captain, had boarded a naval ship and escaped from Vietnam. The defeated warriors shattered the silence with tales of battles. The women evacuated to other corners of the apartment, but we boys sat and listened, half in rapture, half in fright. Late at night, over Johnnie Walker whiskey, the living-room warriors recounted the time when they were young and brave and most alive.

The Captain: "I remember going up Cambodia, Brother, in '71. We killed so many Viet Cong up there we lost count. There was this Mien, and he would kill and kill—crazy for blood—and take out the VC livers and eat them raw....I swear in front of my ancestral grave I know no one more loyal than that guy."

The General: "Viet Cong were everywhere, hidden in the jungle, in the tall bushes. From my helicopter I ordered napalm. You could see the balls of fire brighten the tree line when they exploded. I remember an American adviser friend of mine, killed in a helicopter. *Incroyable!* Blown up by a SAM missile. My own helicopter was shot at by snipers. We landed before it exploded. But we killed many of them that day."

How can such language not stir a child's imagination? America is dull by comparison; it is too real, too impersonal outside the window—a parking lot, a supermarket, Coke machines, the fog drifting harsh and cold. But inside, napalm fire, helicopters exploding, paratroopers landing, bombs oozing out of a drunken warrior's fragmented sentences, transforming the dilapidated apartment into a battleground. Did I not hear the wailing voices of Viet Cong under fire? Did I not see a helicopter burst into flame? Smell the burnt flesh?

Outside our apartment there was a stairwell, dark and cool. The voices echoing from it now—giggling voices trying to be serious—belonged to my cousins and me, four child musketeers, swearing a sacred oath of vengeance after our fathers, drunk, had gone to bed. We talked of eradicating the Viet Cong from the face of the earth.

"With bazookas, with M16s, with kung fu power."

"With Bruce Lee's swiftness and endurance, we can massacre them all."

"We can bomb the levees north of Hanoi during the monsoon," I, the twelve-year-old, the plotter, offered. "We can flood the nasty Viet Cong out to the South China Sea."

In this way the dynamic of the exiled Vietnamese family is formed.

So although I still understand my brother in the coffee shop, while he speaks of vengeance, I have learned a different lesson, the American lesson: the knack of reinventing oneself. To survive in the New World, we must, likewise, challenge the old world's blood-for-blood ethos and search for a new story line.

I am no longer simply Vietnamese. I have changed. I have, like many I know, driven down that hyphen that stretches like a free-way from the mythological kingdom with its one-thousand-year-old ginseng roots toward the cosmopolitan city, the wind in my hair and Springsteen on the radio. English is a bendable language now, English my own song.

I am, for that matter, no longer moved by the old man's martial words on that Guam beach. I believe instead in self-liberation, in American rebirth. But never mind. I am thinking now of those four boys and their fatal gestures and what distinguishes good guys from bad guys in the new Vietnamese American fable.

I am not a Catholic. There is no three-tiered shrine in my family's living room for martyred saints. My mother is a Buddhist but she stopped praying for a time when we lost the war. My father, born a French citizen when Vietnam was a colony, was given a Christian name but never went to church. Unlike the Nguyen brothers, I am only half a Northerner, and I take my cardinal points from the South, from Saigon, my birthplace, where bourgeois sensibilities and Southern irreverence replaces Northern pieties. I have been to Paris and Nice, where my father's relatives live and where—for the first time since leaving Vietnam—I felt, shamelessly, somehow I had come home.

"The Northerners are fanatics," my father said at dinner one night after the Good Guys incident. My father had lived in Paris and liked wine more than jasmine tea; within five years of his arrival in America he had obtained an MBA and lifted us out of poverty into a suburban middle-class life. "The Northerners immolate themselves and talk too readily of martyrdom. They don't think rationally; they think emotionally. *Tu sais, comme ta mère!* Those boys must have ingested all the plots for tragedy from their Northern Catholic parents."

My mother dropped her chopsticks and feigned anger. "We Northerners defeated the French while you drank their wine," she said, but we all laughed. She was, like the rest of us, also drinking French wine. As the entire family sat there under the gaudy faux-crystal chandelier in my parents' five-bedroom house with its kidney-shaped swimming pool, the irony did not escape us: historical tragedy had come to seem beside the point.

How did this happen? Perhaps only a loser knows real freedom. Forced outside of history, away from home and hearth, he can choose to remake himself. One night America seeps in, and out goes the Vietnamese soul of sorrow. For the Vietnamese refugee family, the past is an enigma best left (at least temporarily) alone. Didn't I see America invade the household when the conversation at dinner in our new home leaned slowly but surely toward real estate and escrow, toward jobs and cars and GPAs and overtime and vacation plans—the language of the American Dream? Even my father's dinner conversation had shifted to memories of an earlier time, a time before the war, when B-52 bombs were not falling and Vietnam was a lush tropical paradise or when he was living in Paris as a young man, tempestuously in love.

But I suspect irony was a luxury unavailable to those young men. Without the warriors turned businessmen, the pool, the chandelier above the dining room table to anchor them in a more complex reality, their passions remained colored by Old World vehemence.

A big difference between me and them was that my father, despite his being defined and owned by the past, helped me with my homework. My father, who saw himself as living in exile, nevertheless taught me how to interpret Walter Cronkite's bad news, taught me world history, taught me how to drive.

I did not fail school. That singularly most important American-making institution had embraced me and rejected those boys. I am also nearly seven years older than Loi Nguyen, old enough to record the actual war in my memories as an army brat. I do not need John Woo's slow-mo gore. Because I thought it through myself years ago, I know the illogic of killing Viet Cong from helicopters in peacetime: How would you distinguish them from ordinary Vietnamese? Which conical-hatted figure would you shoot?

A friend who works in the Palawan Refugee Camp in the Philippines recently sent me a poem he found carved on a stone under a tamarind tree. Written by an unknown Vietnamese boat person, it tells how to escape tragedy: "Your mind is like a radio that you can dial to a different voice. It depends on you. So do not keep your mind always tuned to sorrow. If you want, just change the channel."

When I turned thirty recently, years after I switched the dial, as it were, my father said, "At your age I was already a colonel."

"We are very different now, Dad," I snapped, a little irritated. "I don't have a need to be a warrior here in America." My father smiled a sad smile. What relevant words of wisdom can an exiled general pass down to his fully grown American son, the one he sometimes introduces to his ex-army buddies as "the American one," which in Vietnamese could translate, depending on the context, as "bad," "soulless," or "traitorous"?

As I think about those young men and what they did, I realize that I, in Vietnamese eyes, haven't been a very good son. I had denounced my father's passion for his homeland as parochialism, had learned to listen to his war stories as tales of nostalgia, had, in fact, taken the private angst of his generation and disseminated it in public light—an unfilial act.

I imagine the Nguyen brothers adoring their father, the ex-sergeant of the South Vietnamese Army. They must have loved and trusted his war stories. According to the *Sacramento Bee*, the Nguyen brothers had folded their arms—the Vietnamese gesture of filial piety—and asked their parents for permission to leave the house that fateful day. This image haunts me. They tried to bring dignity to their father by fighting his war. They wanted to be good Vietnamese sons: to assuage the old man's grief, the young man must defeat his old man's enemy.

But Hamlet's unfocused vehemence is not to my taste, his bloody rampage to be his father's son inappropriate to the New World. I am more intrigued by the complicated character of Indar in V. S. Naipaul's *A Bend in the River,* who has lost his family home and fortune to political upheavals and been forced outside of territorial boundaries. "I'm a lucky man," he said. "I carry the world within me....I'm tired of being on the losing side....I want to win and win and win."

"To be or not to be" is no longer the question, for some of us Vietnamese children in America have learned to escape the outdated passions. These days, after a weekend visit I hug my mother but cannot approach my father. Instead we regard each other from a distance, nod, and no more. We are veterans from different wars and I have won mine.

A mile or so from the Good Guys store, at the newest plot in St. Mary's Cemetery, flanked by a large statue of St. Pius and an American flag, Long and Pham Nguyen are buried side by side. It takes a while to find their tombstones behind the pink mausoleum. It is late afternoon, and a few birds chirp as the sprinklers spray mist that forms rainbows. The only other visitors at St. Mary's are a Vietnamese family busy burning incense sticks. The smoke, blown by a warm breeze, wavers alluringly.

This desertlike landscape, with it sandalwood fragrance, is not part of Joan Didion's California anymore. The dark epic journeys that end in California have new players. Searching for the Nguyen brothers' tombstones, I find names that leave a kind of phosphorescence on my mind—names like Le, Tran, Vuong, Nguyen— Vietnamese last names that once belonged to emperors of millennia passed, now etched on new tombstones on plots where the grass has not yet fully grown.

Between the two brothers' tombstones I place ginseng roots, $10.99 a box in a Vietnamese grocery store. The box has a plastic cover with the American stars and stripes painted on it. Printed in the lower right-hand corner is the word USA.

National Defeat Day/
National Liberation Day

April 1994

Flipping through my United States passport as if it were a comic book, the customs man at the Noi-Bai Airport, near Hanoi, appeared curious. "Brother, when did you leave Vietnam?"

"Two days before National Defeat Day," I said without thinking. It was an exile's expression, not his.

"God! When did that happen?" asked the man in a comic and exaggerated tone.

"The thirtieth of April, 1975."

"But, Brother," he smiled, "don't you mean National Liberation Day?"

If this conversation had occurred a decade earlier, the difference would have created a dangerous gap between the Vietnamese and the returning Vietnamese American. But this happened a couple of decades after the war had ended, when the walls were down, the borders porous, and as I studied the smiling young official, it occurred to me that there was something about this moment, an epiphany. "Yes, Brother, I suppose I do mean Liberation Day." Not everyone remembers the date with a smile. It marked the Vietnamese Diaspora, boat people, refugees.

On April 28, 1975, my family and I escaped from Saigon in a crowded C-130 cargo plane a few hours before the airport was bombed. We arrived in Guam the next day, in time to hear the BBC's tragic account of Saigon's demise: US helicopters flying over the chaotic city, Viet Cong tanks rolling in, Vietnamese climbing over the gate into the US embassy, boats fleeing down the Saigon River toward the South China Sea.

In time, April 30 became the birth date of an exile's culture, built on defeatism and a sense of tragic ending. For a while, many Vietnamese in America talked of revenge, of blood debts, of the exile's anguish. Their songs had nostalgic titles: "The Day When I Return" and "Oh, Mother Vietnam, We Are Still Here."

April 30, 1976: A child of twelve with nationalistic fervor, I stood in front of San Francisco City Hall with other refugees. I waved the gold flag with three horizontal red stripes. I shouted (to no one in particular), "Give us back South Vietnam!"

April 30, 1979: An uncle told me there was an American plan to retake our homeland by force, "the way Douglas MacArthur did for the South Koreans in the fifties." My eighteen-year-old brother declared that he would join the anticommunist guerrilla movement in Vietnam. My father sighed.

April 30, 1983: I stayed awake all night with Vietnamese classmates from Berkeley to listen to monotonous speeches by angry old men. "National defeat must be avenged by sweat and blood!" one vowed.

But through the years, April 30 has come to symbolize something entirely different to me. Although I sometimes mourn the loss of home and land, it's the American landscape and what it offers that solidify my hyphenated identity. This date of tragic ending, from an optimist's point of view, is also an American rebirth, something close to the Fourth of July.

I remember whispering to a young countryman during one of those monotonous April 30 rallies in the mid-1980s, "Even as the old man speaks of patriotic repatriation we've already become Americans." Assimilation, education, the English language, the American "I"—these have carried me and many others farther from that beloved tropical country than the C-130 ever could. Each optimistic step the young Vietnamese takes toward America is tempered with a betrayal of Little Saigon's parochialism, its sentimentalities, and the old man's outdated passion.

When did this happen? Who knows? One night America quietly seeps in and takes hold of one's mind and body, and the Vietnamese soul of sorrows slowly fades away. In the morning the Vietnamese American speaks a new language of materialism: his vocabulary is peppered with phrases like Mercedez Benz and two-car garage and double income.

My brother never made it to the Cambodian jungle. The would-be guerrilla fighter became instead a civil engineer. My talk of endless possibilities is punctuated with favorite verbs—transcend, redefine, become. "I want to become a writer," I declared to my parents one morning. My mother gasped.

April 30, 1975: Defeat or liberation? "It was a day of joyous victory," said a retired communist official in Hanoi. "We fought and realized Uncle Ho's dream of national independence." Then he asked for Marlboro cigarettes and a few precious dollars. Nhon Nguyen, a real estate salesman in San Jose and a former South Vietnamese naval officer, said: "I could never forget the date. So many people died. So much blood. I could never tolerate communism, you know."

Mai Huong, a young, smartly dressed Vietnamese business-woman in Saigon, had another opinion. Of course it was National Liberation Day, she said. "But it's the South," she told me with a wink, "that liberated the North." Indeed, conservative Uncle Ho has slowly admitted defeat to entrepreneurial and cosmopolitan Miss Saigon. She has taken her meaning from a different uncle, you know, Uncle Sam.

The customs man, on the other hand, stamped my passport and said: "In truth, Brother, there are no winners, no losers. You're lucky, Brother. You left Vietnam and became an American."

April 30, 1993: In the Berkeley hills, in a house that gave to the bay, my Vietnamese American friends and I watched *Gone with the Wind* for the umpteenth time and looked for the scene of our unrequited romantic longings: Scarlett, teary-eyed with wind-blown hair, returning to live in forlorn Tara. She is doing something we no longer can. Or rather, we go only to look and sometimes enter the houses where we once lived, but then we take leave. Children of defeat, self-liberating adults, we hugged instead and, over a couple of bottles of very dry Merlot, recounted to each other our own stories of flight.

The Stories They Carried

December 1994

The image once gripped us—a small boat crowded with Vietnamese refugees bobbing on a vast, merciless sea. From its mast a ragged SOS flag flew while its equally ragged passengers waved thin arms at passing ships. "Help Us. We Love Freedom," their sign said. "We Love USA!"

Once, during the cold war, we couldn't get enough of their stories. Today, as the refugee crisis has become a pandemic, the charm Americans felt at the asylum seeker's naïve enthusiasm for our country has turned into resignation and fear. The thirty-five thousand boat people of Southeast Asia now being sent back to Vietnam have no place in our New World Order narrative.

But stories are all that the refugees possess—all that stand between their freedom and forced repatriation.

In the summer of 1991, as a cub reporter, I found myself with access to a refugee detention center called Whitehead at the western edge of Hong Kong. Journalists were, by and large, barred from entry to this place known for riots and gang fights and mass protests and a handful of self-immolations. There were eleven people, mostly women, who disemboweled themselves in protest of being forced back. The place, divided into sections, is built like a maximum security prison. Barbed wire on top of five-meter-high chicken wire fences.

I got lucky. For several weeks I visited Whitehead (as well as several other refugee centers) as a Vietnamese interpreter for two human rights lawyers. The lawyers represented pro bono a few refugees whose cases, they felt, were strong enough to fight repatriation. No one among the Hong Kong authorities knew I was a journalist.

71

But the refugees knew. The moment I entered the camp, I was swamped. News traveled fast. A journalist got in. He speaks Vietnamese. Talk to him. Tell him your stories.

In many sections I visited I was called a "hero." Several women called me their "savior." I was neither. I was hoping for a story or two. I was sympathetic and hoping, in my own way, to help. I was willing to listen to their stories. And by listening, I was the only source of communication they had with the outside world.

Everyone I met wanted to tell me his or her story. The boat people wanted to convey the injustice they had suffered, first under communist hands and now from Hong Kong authorities in conjunction with the UNHCR—United Nations High Commission on Refugees—who screened them out and deemed them economic refugees ineligible for asylum. Many were called liars when they told of communist atrocities, of oppression back home. In the late eighties, many came from North Vietnam—supposedly the winning side—and forced the international community, in tandem with the UNHCR, to reconsider their asylum policy. They produced the Comprehensive Plan of Action in 1989, which had two key points. The first was to screen all arrivals—to Hong Kong as well as to other ports of asylum—to determine whether the boat people were genuine refugees or, according to the UN Convention, ineligible "economic refugees." The second point was more controversial, entailing the repatriation of those who failed the screening back to their home countries. For the first time since the war had ended, Vietnamese boat people were being repatriated en masse.

It was, of course, much easier for the powers that be to not listen, to label them economic refugees and ship them back, a bunch of liars stripped of their stories at the end of history. The few thousand people in Whitehead Detention Center were all waiting to be sent back. There were apparently two categories, "voluntary repatriates" and "involuntary repatriates."

"Either way," so one old man told me, "all of us are condemned prisoners."

Such certainly will soon be the fate of Diep Tran, a forty-six-year-old former second lieutenant in the South Vietnamese Army

I met in Section 4. Caught while trying to escape in 1979, he was tortured and sent to a reeducation camp while his wife was forced to live with a communist cadre to prevent her family from being blacklisted and sent to the New Economic Zone.

When he and his son finally did reach Hong Kong, he was denied refugee status because he lacked the $3,000 cash demanded by a screening official, he said. In protest, his son, Anh Huy, committed self-immolation in front of the UNHCR official. Tran showed me his son's photos. One is of a smiling teenager. The other is a picture of a burnt, bloodied corpse flanked by grim-looking Vietnamese men.

When he showed me the pictures, Tran's eyes welled up with tears. "I didn't expect him to do this. I didn't escape so that my son would die in front of my eyes."

In another section, Section 8, considered the most unruly of all eleven sections in Whitehead, thirty-eight-year-old Dai Nguyen pulled off his T-shirt and showed me the scars on his back. The scars described years of cruelty in a reeducation camp. But they failed to convince the screening officer of his political past. "I have no papers with me. No one told me that I had to have proof besides what I carry on my back." He was waiting to be repatriated. On top of the barrack, someone had torn up a piece of tin and painted a picture of Lady Liberty holding her torch. Hanging on the wall of another was a sign written in blood: "Freedom Or Death." In that same barrack, a teenager had tattooed Lady Liberty's face onto his own chest, using ink from a pen, a needle, and a little mirror.

Huong Nguyen, 43, a haggard-looking woman, spent ten years as a forced laborer in the New Economic Zone clearing jungle and watching her fellow laborers get blown to bits by land mines. She was pregnant and had a one-year-old child. Her husband, a South Vietnamese lieutenant, had been killed while trying to escape from a reeducation camp. She had tried to escape in 1985 with her sons but wound up separated from them. In the end, the sons arrived in Hong Kong before the cutoff date of June 16, 1988, after which all arrivals had to be screened to qualify as political refugees. Although her sons arrived in time, she came on a different boat, too late, and was screened out.

Lam A Lu was a Montagnard tribesman who fought for the United States and was sent to hard labor camp where he was tortured before he escaped. Hong Kong authorities judged his story a lie and denied him asylum, despite the seven bullet wounds in his body.

If A Lu and Tran—both meeting the criteria required of political asylum seekers—were rejected, their fellow detainees wondered in despair, who could get accepted? Certainly not the Buddhist monk in Section 6 who fled Vietnam because he was forbidden to perform ceremonies in the rural area; nor the Catholic nun who was punished for singing Catholic songs. And certainly not a number of men and women who had worked for the US armed forces as interpreters or office workers during the war.

The stories are endless, each one more tragic than the next. For these storytellers, the end of their story was this: the free world no longer exists.

Were it not for the cruelty of the joke, Huong Nguyen might find her story laughable. A woman who laughed easily despite her circumstances, she said, "I ran out of tears. So now I just laugh when I can." Her sons, who share the same history as their mother, now live in Santa Ana, California. Their mother, on the other hand, has become a "living ghost."

When forced repatriation began in July 1989 it provoked an international uproar. A few years later, it has become international acceptance. Britain, running Hong Kong for a few years yet, even signed a treaty with Vietnam making repatriation of the Hong Kong people possible.

The stateless population, in the meantime, is growing. More and more are born into no-man's-land. Hong Kong refugee camps have one of the highest birthrates in the world.

Consider the children. Refugee children know next to nothing about policies regarding them. Although stateless the moment they opened their eyes, like children anywhere else they played where they could, and in the afternoon at Whitehead their laughter rang out.

Yet, it is hard to imagine a happy childhood in such a desolate place. Theirs is a world of chicken wings in red plastic buckets, wet, gooey rice in rusted tin pails, bunk beds that sheltered whole families, tick bites and rashes, unbearable temperatures, and odious stench. Under oppressive corrugated-roof hangars in punishing humid summer heat often reaching 100 degrees, people ate and slept. Fights broke out regularly and every few weeks or so someone would hang him or herself in the latrines. In the camps, hurried and banal and careless sex went on behind flimsy, ragged curtains next to which children played hopscotch or sang.

High overhead jumbo jets soared across the Hong Kong sky, going to who knows where. But for a child born in one the camps the plane might as well belong to a world of fantasy. His world is grounded to a reality that is defined by smallness, and the borders of his country are made of chicken wire fences, ones he cannot cross. One child who had never lived in a real house, never, for that matter, seen one with his own eyes, referred to the bunk bed he shared with his family of four as "my house."

A scene came back to me recently and I was surprised that I could have forgotten it. One late afternoon in Whitehead a group of children were trying to retrieve a bright red wildflower growing a few feet outside the fence by using a thin stick of firewood. Nature was all around the center, the sea sparkled and gleamed, but it was all out of reach. I remember a guard standing outside the fence watching, idly smoking a cigarette while the children tried in vain to retrieve the flower.

I had told myself I would get those kids some flowers the next time I came back into the camp but then, so busy taking notes and listening to people with life and death stories, I simply forgot.

"Is it true, Uncle," a child about seven asked me one early morning, "that at the red light you stop and at the green light you go?" Other boys were listening intently. They had been betting—with what I didn't know—as to who was right. Born inside the camps, they had never seen traffic lights before, except on the TV in the communal cafeteria.

"You go when it's green," I told them. "You stop when it's red."

For the West the lesson about itself is sobering. Our compassion for those who fled from our enemies' territories—President Reagan, who saw himself as someone who had defeated communism, in his farewell speech recalled a Vietnamese boat person calling out to an American sailor, "Hey, Freedom Man" before being rescued—turned into what everyone now begins to call fatigue.

We suffer from compassion fatigue, the pundits tell us. There are too many refugees. Haitians. Cubans. Afghans. Tibetans. Chinese. You name it. Don't you know the borders have melted? The West frets. Lady Liberty turns her back. Too many love the USA. Too many love freedom. It is not necessarily, in the final analysis, a good thing in the post–cold war era.

A refugee from a communist country once had a role in the story Americans told themselves. He who risked his life jumping over the barbed wire fence in Berlin or sailed across the treacherous sea from Vietnam to search for freedom reassured those at the end of the exodus trail that the American way of life represented something worth having, that they lived on the right side of the cold war divide.

Once, the West readily opened its arms to these poor souls to validate the myth, and to score political points in their constant vigilance against communism. *Give us your tired, your poor, your huddled masses…*

Overnight, so now it seems, refugees and illegal immigrants and migrant workers and even the domestic homeless have melted into an indistinguishable blur. Recoiling from our earlier idealism, we Americans tell ourselves homelessness is now an inherent part of the New Disorderly World and something out of our control.

As it is, "the outside of Vietnam," Diep Tran told me, sighing, "has become the same as the inside of Vietnam. You have no rights if you are homeless and countryless. You don't even have the rights to your own story, your own words."

"Hong Kong simply has had enough with refugees," said Duyen Nguyen, a Vietnamese American in his late thirties who is a deputy director for the US Joint Volunteer Program in Hong Kong. A consummate fighter for refugee rights, Duyen always looked tired. As he talked to me he took off his thick glasses and looked out the window of his office to the crowded, mildew-stained buildings in Kowloon, where Hong Kong Chinese lived in tiny spaces. Descendants from refugees of another war, their colorful laundry hung on the wires of every tiny balcony like a thousand Marc Rothko paintings. "Besides, there is pressure to get rid of the problem by the time China takes over in 1997," he added.

The United Nations High Commission for Refugees, according to several disaffected former staff members, has capitulated to the process because it believes the only way to solve the problem is to make life so difficult for the Vietnamese refugees that they would rather volunteer to go home. "In fact, forced repatriation is working—the number of asylum seekers has dropped dramatically," said a former UNHCR staff member. "Forget human rights and compassion—the bottom line is to find a quick fix for the refugee crisis."

In the *South China Morning Post,* letters to the editors are mostly anti-refugee to the point of being rabid. After almost two decades, Hong Kong is fed up. One resident urged that "Vietnamese people should be sent to labor camps to work as slaves." Other letters suggested Hong Kong should force everyone back to Vietnam regardless of screening. These are presumably the same people who are themselves searching frantically for visas out of Hong Kong before China takes power in 1997.

These days no one will speak up for the Vietnamese refugees in Hong Kong or, for that matter, the refugees scattered in various camps in Southeast Asia, but perhaps that is beside the point. The boat people, kicking and screaming as they are carted off to airplanes for the journey home, warn us that maybe it is also our misfortune that we can no longer hear them. Our own idealism wanes; we too, like them, sit in the dark, our hands on our ears, poor, huddled masses.

On the bunk bed where he stored all that he owned, where he wrote and slept and ate with his wife and two kids, Lieu Tran, 31, offered me lunch. One afternoon we sat cross-legged with the curtain drawn and had fried chicken wings—a staple here in the camp—along with porridge.

"I just got my second chicken wing last week," he said matter-of-factly. This expression is something of an in-house joke. You get your first "chicken wing" when you receive a letter from the Hong Kong immigration authorities informing you that you have failed your interview with immigration officials—that you have been deemed an "economic refugee." You are allowed to appeal to the court under the UNHCR's observation. When you get your second chicken wing it means your appeal has come back and, if the answer is still no, you're out of luck. With two chicken wings, Lieu said, laughing, "you can fly home to communist paradise."

Below Lieu's pillow were stacks of notebooks and letters. Life in the camp had given him plenty of time to reflect. His whole life, he said, had bled into these notebooks and letters—"an autobiography of a stateless man," he called it. He took one out and said, "If you could publish this in America I would really appreciate it."

I was tempted to write something about Lieu's life, but having read the following letter, I thought it best if he told it himself, translated here in full:

"This letter I write to you in the free world begging for help. You can lend your voice and scream for us, we who scream constantly but are never heard. You who live on stable ground can reach out to a people who live on the edge of an abyss.

"I grew up in the city of Hue, Vietnam. My father served in the South Vietnamese Army during the war as a sergeant. He was shot and killed by the Viet Cong in September 1973 while on his way home on leave.

"After 1975, South Vietnam fell into the hands of the communists. The communist regime began to confiscate our property and put many of us on trial. Because my father was in the army, my family was tried for having committed 'crimes against the Party and the People.'

"We owed them, our accusers said, for our 'crimes of blood.' In January 1978 we were forced to leave Hue for the high mountain wilderness in Dac Lac, an area the communists call the New Economic Zone.

"How we suffered! Those years in the NEZ we were slaves. Each day we went into the forests to clear brush. We planted vegetables, which got taxed by the state so we had little left. We had to survive on tree roots and yams.

"We suffered diseases and many accidents. There was no medicine. Many who were sent there with me died slowly from malaria. There were no schools, no churches, no temples. We had nowhere to turn.

"My siblings and I couldn't take it anymore and we fled. In the city we begged on the streets and worked as coolies and tried to avoid government officers who would send us back to the NEZ if they found us.

"We thought that if life in Vietnam continued this way, we would die slowly. In 1988, my sister, my wife, my little daughter, and I escaped from Vietnam. Our boat was made of bamboo, and with thirty others we sailed out to sea. Some of us died of thirst, some of starvation, but at least the dead found peace at the bottom of the sea. It was better this way—to risk becoming fish bait for a chance of freedom.

"Those who survived among us arrived in Hong Kong after twenty-five days. Immediately we were placed in a detention center called Thai-A-Chau. We lived on cement floor like animals. Each of us got two bowls of rice daily. In winter we went without blankets. Our daily lives consisted of waiting in food lines and trying to protect ourselves from beatings by the Hong Kong police.

"A year after I arrived in Hong Kong I was screened for my refugee status. The interpreter, who was Chinese, did not speak Vietnamese very well. The screening officer did not allow me to explain but only to answer questions. When I said something he didn't like, he shouted at me. 'You're a liar,' he screamed.

"The worst thing was that he would not write down important events about my past so that the court could see that I was truly a political refugee. All was lost when a letter came back to my barracks informing me that I was an 'economic migrant'—ineligible for asylum. My family and I live in constant fear of repatriation, afraid of having to return to the prison of communist Vietnam.

"Our home these last months has been a place called Whitehead Detention Center. Life has gotten worse for people who live here. Some have gone crazy because of the crowded conditions; others have gotten sick because there is so little medicine. A few I know have committed suicide. I fear most for the children. What future is there for children who live without a place to play, who live behind an iron fence?

"Vietnam and the United Kingdom have agreed to return all boat people from Hong Kong to Vietnam. Facing that impending action, we live in anguish and pain. But my family and I have agreed to this: we are determined to commit mass suicide here in Hong Kong, if necessary, rather than return to Vietnam where one has no right to be human.

"Perhaps you Americans can recognize in us a kindred people who treasure freedom more than life."

The screening process Hong Kong uses to determine which Vietnamese fit political refugee status is controversial and has been condemned by Amnesty International and the Lawyers' Committee for Human Rights. Many interpreters are Chinese immigrants from Vietnam who can't speak Vietnamese very well. The people aren't allowed to tell their stories. The process has declared that fewer than 8 percent of the boat people are eligible for political asylum, a number that has stayed consistent for months, suggestive of a quota. The rest are to be shipped home.

I asked Lieu if he knew the difference between involuntary repatriation and voluntary repatriation. "Those too weak to fight when the police raid this place for potential repatriates will be termed voluntary," he answered. "Those of us who fight to the death will be called involuntary."

Then he showed me his knife. He had taken a metal bar that once supported his bunk bed and rubbed it onto the cement floor until it had become a kind of sharp swing blade. "I will never go home," he said and gripped it until his knuckles turned white.

In Section 6 a woman named Xuan Le, who had the look of someone malnourished for years, told me how she and her family nearly drowned while escaping from Hai Phong Province. In her mid-forties, she looked ten years older, her face darkened by the sun, the wrinkles deep, her shoulder blades protruding. She stood about five feet tall, weighing no more than ninety pounds. Her hair had turned almost all gray.

"One night my family and I decided to escape. There were three of us in my family. My husband was still in a reeducation camp.

My sister lives in Canada. She sent money home and I kept saving until I had enough to buy seats on the boat. I took my two little boys and left from Hai Phong in the middle of the night.

"A few days out and our boat hit a coral reef. God, it was so terrifying. Water started to rise. Children were crying. It was winter. The sea was ice cold. It began to sink.

"I stood there for maybe eight to ten hours. The water went slowly up to my knees, then my waist. My two children, I would not let the water touch them. One hung onto my neck and the smaller one sat on my shoulders....

"I don't know how I got my strength. I thought we were going to die. Everyone on the boat thought so too. People started praying. But I just stood. I didn't move at all. I would die first before my children, I decided. I turned into stone."

Then a miracle happened to Xuan Le. A Hong Kong patrol boat came by and rescued the despondent refugees. As the patrolmen pulled her and her children out of the freezing water, Xuan Le said she couldn't feel her own body at all. "I was no longer human. I was something else. It took a week or so before I had feeling in my fingers again. It was...it was as if I had turned into Hon Vong Phu," recalled the gray-haired woman, laughing hysterically.

Up in the coastal province of Quang Ninh there was a rock in the shape of a woman holding a child. It was called Hon Vong Phu—the Rock Waiting for Her Husband. According to legend, the stone figure had once been a real woman. A thousand years ago, as she awaited the return of her war-faring husband who was most likely never to return, a thunderstorm turned her and the baby in her arms into stone. Over time she became a local goddess, and villagers and fishermen prayed to her for good weather.

I told Mrs. Xuan that she was very brave. But she shook her head adamantly. "Look around you," she said and gestured toward the squatting women washing their children by the washing area out in the bright cement courtyard. "Tell me which Vietnamese mother would react differently?"

Save me! Save us!
You're our savior.

You are our only hope.

There is a famous photo of two Vietnamese women screaming for help from behind white metal bars. It was taken on December 12, 1989, in Hong Kong. One woman has her hands outstretched; the other, on her knees, wearing a white headband, prays.

A couple of hours after this picture was taken, the two women, their families, and other inmates from the Phoenix House Detention Center—fifty-one people in all—were sent back to Vietnam against their will, flown by Cathay Pacific Airlines.

The main reason I was sent to Hong Kong was because forced repatriation not only affected the thirty-five thousand Vietnamese boat people living in refugee camps across Southeast Asia but all of the thirty million internationally displaced persons now scattered across the globe. It was becoming a universally accepted practice.

But I also went because of that picture. For days I couldn't get it out of my head after I first saw it, especially the image of the praying woman, her white headband, and the way she looked into the camera. The white headband is the Vietnamese funeral garment. Vietnam's national forehead, one might even say, is bound with this white strip of cloth. Over the years it has become this woman's unofficial flag—her symbol of suffering, of struggle, of death.

When I first saw the photo I immediately thought of my mother: it could have been her. It could have been us.

The photo brought back painful memories. One afternoon in the refugee camp in Guam, my mother came back to our tent with her clothes all wet and her eyes full of tears. The American GIs had built the shower stalls without roofs, and while the women took their showers the GIs parked their army truck next to the stalls and stood atop the hoods and watched. Water was rationed; there was no second chance. Mother bit her lips and took the shower with her clothes on.

Another time, a GI tossed a quarter at me. I bent to pick it up from the muddy ground, despite my better judgment, trying not to look at his face. I had come from an upper-class family in Vietnam. I had seen urchins begging on the streets of Saigon. When I came back to our tent and gave the coin to my mother she looked at me astonished. But she did not say anything and took the coin. I don't remember saying anything either. Just the same, we recognized the look in each other's face: shame and humiliation.

I went to Hong Kong not knowing what I would find, but I knew what I felt: rage against the treatment of boat people, rage against the West. I had wanted to do something. I had wanted to help. But I went not purely out of my own piousness. There was no denying it: a cub reporter, I jumped at the rare opportunity. I had connections and I knew I was going to be the only American journalist who spoke Vietnamese there and, therefore, could get into the notorious Whitehead Detention Center as an interpreter. That fact was, despite everything else, thrilling throughout my time in Hong Kong: me, going undercover, alone, watching an important post–cold war story unfold.

What I hadn't prepared for, however, was that I was too close to the story. Go back a few years and it could easily be me mired in this camp. Worse, throughout my presence in that detention center, I was bewildered. I had no clear sense of where my true alliance lay, where exactly I stood. Was I an activist, an interpreter, or a journalist? So many people with so many stories and I was the only receptacle for their tragedies. I was dizzy, and each time I entered that camp I felt like I was drowning in their sorrow and sadness.

What was the true nature of my relationship with the boat people?

I was both connected and disconnected from the refugee's narrative. My experience belonged to the cold war story, one where I fled the oncoming communist army and was taken in by a generous America. I lived the American Dream, grew up as an American in an American suburb, and graduated from a good university. I went on further. I fancied myself a writer. I saw myself living a cosmopolitan life, a premise of ever expanding opportunity and choices.

The boat people who fled after the cold war ended, on the other hand, left Vietnam too late. And all over the world the business of protecting refugees has turned into the business of protecting the West from asylum seekers themselves. Movement toward resettlement countries, UN officials will now tell you, is movement in "the wrong direction."

Perhaps nowhere else but among Vietnamese refugees lost in no-man's-land and facing deportation would a Vietnamese from America, however deep his sympathy, however fierce his rage, cease to simply be a Vietnamese. He confronts a crucial self-realization: he is no longer a refugee, no longer an inheritor of one set of history.

83

In America I had nurtured a hidden psychic wound, a stigma to which I had uncritically attached myself and, over the years, I wore it like a scar or a badge of honor. I had seen myself as a refugee living in America. I was obsessed with my own story, my expulsion from my own homeland. Among those whose future was as dark as that of a condemned prisoner facing a firing squad, I was made keenly aware that I had been self-indulgent. They may love the USA but the USA can no longer afford to love them. I, who left Vietnam earlier as a child, on the other hand, have been generously embraced by the West and have, in turn, embraced it.

The refugee sobriquet no longer fits. I was a free man, someone who grew up in California, took vacations to Europe and Mexico, someone who attended a prestigious university, someone with an American passport, a press pass, and various credit cards that, in an age where borders are becoming increasingly porous, seem to open every door and customs gate.

Indeed, after a few weeks in Hong Kong, confronted with the boat people's profound grief, I began to miss my friends in America, my life in America. I felt that I began to tense up each time I walked through the barbed wire gate while the armed Chinese guards gave me dirty looks. Looking back I realized that I had unconsciously made the point of looking different from the boat people. I dressed impeccably. I ironed my shirt. I could not have possibly been mistaken as a boat person were a riot to break out and the Hong Kong police had to come in with their batons and tear gas.

I was no savior, no hero. I wasn't even sure how much, as a writer, I could help. If anything, I was, in stealth, trying to save myself from them.

Among almost all the people I met and deeply admired—Hung Tran, Pam Baker, Duyen Nguyen, Quyen Vuong, Phu Bui, and many more—lawyers, social workers, NGO (non-governmental organization) officials, scholars, and so on—people who dedicated months if not years of their lives to helping the boat people in Hong Kong, there was almost a pallid pall that hung over their lives. They lived and breathed refugee policies. Boat people's cases piled up high on their desks. They took tragedies home with them.

But even if compassion fatigue hadn't defeated them, it was at least wearing them down. Duyen Nguyen, for instance, rarely cracked a smile and I never once heard him laugh. Quyen, a Fulbright scholar, was informed by her own journey as a boat person, but her smile was infinitely sad. Others—volunteers, workers for NGOs who returned to help—bickered among themselves, disagreed as to which was the best tactic to help those facing deportation. One night at a hush-hush secret meeting between social workers and lawyers and NGO workers who had wanted to go beyond their professional capacities to help the boat people's causes, one man just plain lost it, stood up and screamed, then promptly stomped out.

If they agreed on anything at all, it was that I was a lightweight, a fly-by-night sort who came in for a story and no more, whereas they…they were entrenched. They had chosen their battle. I, though sympathetic, hadn't chosen mine. I was merely a visitor to the front line. By gathering and disseminating news from the inside, I might be able to be of some help, but by all estimates, considering how global generosity has dwindled in the face of millions upon millions of stateless people, not by much.

I had initially wanted to dissuade them of that notion, but soon I came to accept that it was true. I didn't want to be consumed like a Duyen Nguyen or like that unrivaled champion of refugees Pam Baker, attorney at law, who worked tirelessly and who didn't seem to need sleep or food, just cigarettes. I was, less than a month into the fight—and I hated to admit it at the time—already tired and worn out. I brightened up one morning when the phone rang and my office told me that my assignment to Europe in the spring had been approved. I couldn't wait to leave. Lightweight indeed.

There's more. I slept badly at night in my hotel room throughout my time in Hong Kong and had horrid, vivid dreams. The summer heat was getting to me. In the center, I was getting tick bites, rashes. I never got used to the fetid smell of the entire place.

The division between Northerners and Southerners who did not trust each other made the situation worst, and many fights that broke out were due to this century-old demarcation. Gangs referred to as "bear heads" by the internees were also a problem, as Vietnam released its worst elements and let them escape and Hong Kong authorities allowed them to mix with the various sections as a way to create unrest and disorganization. Though I could not confirm it, rape was reportedly occurring in the camp with impunity, and though no one would talk about it, young women without men were free for all.

There was a kind pettiness among some of the people in the center that greatly irked me. A few times, when I had listened to someone for too long, another would come along and say, "His story is not as good as mine. He lies. I don't lie. Let me tell you mine." It was as if I was the UNHCR official myself and could decide on their fates.

One windless afternoon I nearly passed out. It was right before Dai Nguyen had wanted me to touch his scars, as if to validate what I saw with my other senses. "Touch them," he said and I smiled and shook my head no. "That's okay. I believe you, Brother." I suddenly realized that until that moment I had been holding my breath.

And so, if I left for Hong Kong with rage against the West for closing its doors on the boat people, I was coming back with more or less the same rage but with one caveat, a self-knowledge I didn't expect: I was having compassion fatigue of my own.

On my last day in Whitehead a young woman named Tuyet wanted to talk with me. I had talked to her before and she had asked if I could send letters she'd written to friends in America on her behalf, a request to which I'd said yes.

Within earshot of several young women friends of hers, Tuyet asked for another favor. "Do you think I'm pretty?" she began.

"Yes," I answered politely. She hadn't really stood out among her friends; average was my assessment. It occurred to me as I said this, however, that she was wearing makeup, which was unusual in the center.

"Would you marry me?" she asked softly. Her voice had perceptibly changed. She was trembling. "Save me, Brother, please," she whispered. "If you marry me, I won't be sent back. Save me. I'll be your servant for the rest of my life."

The night before, the women in Section 6 were tearing white cloths for headbands and some were sharpening knives fashioned out of metal bars pulled from their bunk beds. There were rumors of an impending raid to take more people back. As far as many were concerned they were being ushered back to their own funeral, and they were not going without a fight.

I looked at Tuyet. She couldn't have been more than twenty. If I can't save them all, why not just one? Others have done it. New brides have walked out of this barbed wire prison on the arms of their NGO worker-heroes while the rest looked on with envy and awe.

For a few seconds, under the burning sun, I hesitated. I didn't say anything. I kept looking at her. It felt as if the culmination of my own confusion and conflict seemed to have come to rest at this juncture.

In my mind's eye I saw a fading ghost of myself saying yes. I saw another narrative taking place other than the one I was after. Tuyet and I would be married. We would stay and fight the good fight. Then, when it was all over, I would take my new bride home to America, to glorious California, the Golden State, the ultimate destination for all refugees, to see my family, and beyond that the events were invisible and innumerable, beyond my imagination.

Then, just like that, I started to break out in a cold sweat. I saw my own future as dead-ended as her own. Instead of doing the story I was sent to Hong Kong to do, I would end up married to it. It was not a narrative that I had imagined for myself. And it was not what I had given up going to medical school and picked up the pen for. I had yearned to be free from the past. This was why I had become a writer, wasn't it? Or, was this—the past, the war, its aftermath—the story I was ready to tell and, by saying yes to Tuyet, willing to live with for the rest of my life?

In the end, I was both a coward and, typical of myself in the face of someone else's great distress, indecisive. I became helpless. In retrospect, I dearly wish I had been deliberate instead of circum-spect and just said no. Instead, I told a lie. "I am so tired, Tuyet. Listen, I'll come in tomorrow and we'll talk then, all right?"

Tuyet smiled and thanked me profusely as I walked out of the center for the last time. I felt her stare on my back from behind the chicken wire fence. I was sure she was beaming. I dared not look back. In my hesitation, I had given her false hope.

And no, I am not unaware that I had become a bit like the West itself; the West, that is, writ very, very small.

* * *

Mid-flight back to San Francisco, I woke from a dream in which many indistinguishable dark faces from behind barbed wire fences stared out at me. I saw those laughing children playing hide-and-seek among the barracks, their bare, dirty little feet slapping against the cement surface of the courtyard. It was an early dawn and out the plane's window, far down below, the Pacific Ocean glowed like an iridescent mirror while above it my plane softly hummed and soared. Why is it some can travel back and forth over its vast expanse with ease and others die trying to traverse its treacherous waters? And what are the moral obligations of a free man to his countrymen who are not?

I had no easy answers. I still live with the questions.

On the plane, the backpack on which I rested my feet was bulging with unpublished biographies and poems and letters that people had entrusted to me. They could not very well take them back to Vietnam or these stories and testimonies would, ironically, be counted as evidence against the state, reasons enough for imprisonment, or worse. Vietnam was the only country willing to use the boat people's biographies verbatim against them.

But having read many of their stories I realized they offered me no answers, only added to my sense of guilt for having survived, for being what one religious gray-haired woman in the center called me, "the blessed one." The stewardess who tapped me on the shoulder to offer me various choices of drinks was as startled as I when I turned from the window: my face was full of tears.

The boat people once raced toward the promised land when the iron curtain still divided the world, and it was understood that risking one's life to be free was a good thing. But the myth ended midway in their flight. Their misfortune was not that they were liars but that history, having taken a sharp turn around a bend, made liars of them.

Hon Vong Phu, so I read recently, had crumbled and fallen into the ocean. The stone woman and her child, broken into many fragments, are scattered now on the ocean floor. Their curse, released at last, clings to the fleeing people of Vietnam.

They Shut the Door on My Grandmother

August 1991

When someone dies in the convalescent home where my grand-mother lives, the nurses rush to close all the patients' doors. Though as a policy death is not to be seen at the home, she can always tell when it visits. The series of doors being slammed shut reminds her of the firecrackers during Tet.

The nurses' efforts to hide death are more comical to my grand-mother than reassuring. "Those old ladies die so often," she quips in Vietnamese, "every day is like New Year."

Still, it is lonely to die in such a place. I imagine some wasted old body under a white sheet being carted silently through the empty corridor on its way to the morgue. While in America a person may be born surrounded by loved ones, in old age one is often left to take the last leg of life's journey alone.

Perhaps that is why my grandmother talks mainly now of her hometown, Bac-Lieu, in the Mekong Delta. Its river and rice fields are vivid in her retelling. Having lost everything during the war, she can now offer me only her distant memories: life was not disjointed back home; one lived in a quiet harmony with the land; people died in their homes surrounded by neighbors and relatives. And no one shut your door.

So it goes...The once gentle, connected world of the past is but the language of dreams. In this fast-paced society of chaotic lives, we are swept along and have little time left for spiritual comfort. Instead of relying on neighbors and relatives, on the river and land, we hope the health care system won't let us down in our old age.

Instead of going to temple to pray for good health, we pay life and health insurance.

My grandmother's children and grandchildren share a certain pang of guilt. After a stroke paralyzed her, we could no longer keep her at home. And although we visit her regularly, we are not living up to the filial piety standard expected of us in the old country. My father silently grieves and my mother suffers from headaches when they visit. (Does my mother see herself, I wonder, in such a home in a decade or two?)

Once, a long time ago, living in Vietnam, we used to stare death in the face. The war, in many ways, had heightened our sensibilities toward living and dying. I saw dead bodies when I was five after a battle erupted near my house during the Tet Offensive. I remember holding onto my great uncle's hand as we watched blue bottle flies gather on the wounds of the dead. If I had been afraid, I now feel appreciative of my great uncle's gesture: he taught me to look the horror of war in the face.

Though the fear of death and dying is a universal one, Vietnamese do not hide from it. We pray daily to the dead at our ancestral altar. We talk to ghosts. Death pervades our poems, novels, and sad-ending fairy tales. We dwell in its tragedy. We know that terrible things can and do happen to ordinary people.

But if agony and pain and suffering are part of Vietnamese culture, even to the point of being morbid, pleasure is at the center of American culture. While Vietnamese holidays are based on death anniversaries of famous kings and heroes, here we celebrate birth dates of presidents.

American popular culture treats death with humor. People laugh and scream at blood-and-guts movies. Zombie flicks are the rage. The wealthy sometimes freeze their dead relatives. Cemeteries are places of business, complete with colorful brochures. There are, I saw on TV the other day, drive-by funerals in some places in the Midwest where you don't have to get out of your car to pay your respects to the deceased.

That America relies upon the pleasure principle and happy endings in its entertainments does not, however, assist us in evading suffering. Americans tell their kids everything will be okay. American children are spoon-fed undaunted optimism and happily-ever-afters, but they then have to confront realities like divorce, domestic violence, drugs, broken homes, and failed politicians. No wonder so many teenagers, as if chasing the saccharine taste of childhood narratives, seek solace in the pages of Stephen King and Anne Rice, horror's king and queen. These days the Little Engine that Could carries very few passengers.

Then there is the loneliness of old age. When one visits the convalescent home, the suffering of the old is self-evident. There is an old man, once an accomplished concert pianist, now rendered helpless by senility and arthritis. Every morning he sits in his wheelchair and stares at the piano in the cafeteria. One feeble woman in her late nineties who outlived all of her children keeps repeating, "My son will take me home. My son will take me home." One smells death in the air even if one cannot see it there. One hears death in the moans and groans of those in pain. Take a look down the hall. There are those mindless, bedridden bodies kept alive with an assortment of tubes and pulsating machines.

Last week on her eighty-third birthday I went to see my grandmother. She smiled her sweet, sad smile.

"Where will you end up in your old age?" she asked.

I was taken aback by the question. The memories of the monsoon rain and the tropical sun and a world of clanship and an insular network of people came back to mind. Not here, not here, I wanted to tell her. But the soft moaning of a patient next door and the smell of alcohol wafting from the sterile corridor brought me back to reality.

"Anywhere is fine, Grandma," I told her instead, trying to keep up with her courageous spirit. "All I'm asking for is that they don't shut my door."

My Vietnam, My America

December 1990

Sometimes the following scene emerges from my Vietnamese childhood: I am sitting in a slow-moving jeep watching Christmas lights
flashing from an old thatched roof under which a GI bargains with
a Saigon bar girl in a green miniskirt. I hear the murmur of wet
tires on the flooded road, the GI's laughter, and the girl's flirting
curses. The deal is struck. The soldier's strong foreign cologne
wafts in the air. His hand reaches for her. She, cursing still, gears
herself for the embrace.

Uncle Sam's soldiering nephew slept once with Miss Saigon,
and in the morning both had changed. One goes home haunted by
a turbulent love affair, the other, in the aftermath of her tragic
ending, dreams of a new beginning in America. If Vietnam has
become, to Americans, a buzzword for ill-fought wars, a metaphor
for disaster, America has become, to the Vietnamese, the symbol of
freedom and happiness. Yes, Vietnam is independent at last. But the
Vietnamese, impoverished and oppressed, are far from happiness.

Last spring when I visited Hong Kong's Whitehead Detention
Center, some Vietnamese detainees showed me a statue of Lady
Liberty made out of tin. They said she symbolized their aspiration
toward freedom. Badly copied and smeared by rain, she stood four
feet tall on the rooftop of Barrack 24, Section 8, shaking in the wind
like an old banana leaf.

"America?" said a teenager in Section 8, too young to remember
the Vietnam War but old enough to have fought in and escaped
from the war in Cambodia, where Vietnam was the invader.
"America is paradise." And, he speculated in his Hanoi accent,

"There are no sufferings in America." It is true—from a fleeing refugee's point of view. America becomes everything Vietnam can't be; it is open to interpretation. In America you can avoid Khmer Rouge mines that blow your legs off and reduce you to begging on Saigon's sidewalks. In America there are no reeducation camps and malaria-infested New Economic Zones where you are forced to grow yams and corn from the hard, bitter soil.

"In America," a Vietnamese who recently arrived in the United States writes home to his impoverished cousins, "you can cook without fire, get money from machines, send letters over telephone wires, watch the world via satellites, drive for kilometers on well-paved roads. In America your children grow taller, smarter, more handsome. Best of all, the government leaves you alone."

In the dark of night, thousands of Vietnamese climb on board old fishing boats for the perilous journey toward the American GI's wondrous home.

Uncle Sam's soldiering nephew, on the other hand, came home traumatized. Now when Americans speak of foreign ventures we are more prudent. The painful memories of Vietnam come back to haunt us and we instinctively ask, "Is it going to be another Vietnam?" Vietnam, in effect, has become a vault filled with tragic metaphors for every American to use.

Ho Chi Minh, the My Lai Massacre, Kent State, Saigon, Hanoi, the Domino Theory: those, among other names, places, and catchphrases, are listed in the book *Cultural Literacy: What Every American Needs to Know,* by E. D. Hirsch Jr. But what *does* every American know? Americans shrug. Vietnam is an unhealed wound, the stuff bad dreams are made of, a legacy of defeat and shame. And so on.

"When Americans say 'Vietnam', they don't mean Vietnam," my uncle complains. He once served as a pilot in the Vietnamese Air Force, flying C-130 cargo planes. Americans don't take defeat and bad memories very well, he says. They try to escape them. Americans make a habit of blaming small countries for the bad things that happen to the United States: cocaine from Colombia, AIDS from Haiti, a nasty flu from Hong Kong, hurricanes from the Caribbean.

But Vietnam—Vietnam is special. What Henry Kissinger described as a "fourth-rate power" had cracked the ivory tower and plagued the American psyche; that hell in a very small place had devastated the bright and shiny citadel. For the first time in history, Americans were caught in the past, haunted by unanswerable questions, confronted with a tragic ending.

But never fear: Hollywood comes to the rescue. It is free with its various interpretations. *Apocalypse Now* describes an American's mythical adventure in a tropic jungle where he confronts other Americans who have been transformed into insane barbarians. *The Deer Hunter* shows a game of Russian roulette being played out for money between an American and some Vietnamese, suggesting Americans and Vietnamese are equally crazy. Insanity explains away otherwise complicated plots and is what we plead in America when we commit hideous crimes. *Tour of Duty* returns to the metaphor of the brutal embrace: Uncle Sam's nephews raping Miss Saigon and then blowing her brains out. Sylvester Stallone carried the war one step further. As Rambo shooting down faceless Vietnamese and sleeping with the beautiful and mysterious Miss Saigon, Stallone led us to believe that he had single-handedly won the lost war for America and restored its pride. Audiences cheered him on.

I know a Vietnamese man who makes money acting in Hollywood. He had survived the war and the perilous journey on the South China Sea to come to America, and now he plays Viet Cong, ARVN (Army of the Republic of Vietnam) soldiers, civilians. He is a great actor, but no one recognizes his face. Time and again he dies, spurting fake blood from his torso and heart. At other times he screams in pain, reinterpreting his own past. "Hollywood loves me," he jokes. "I die well."

Watching such movies, Vietnamese old enough to remember the war giggle uncomfortably. These naïve interpretations of the conflict little resemble their own past. Vietnam was a three-sided war, with North and South at each other's throats, but in the retelling, America has appropriated itself as the central figure in an otherwise complex narrative. Some are enraged, but many are resigned. What they know and won't admit to the American audience is that for them history is a series of personal impressions. Fact and details and analysis and fancy interpretations can't capture the truth about Vietnam any more than wildly fabricated war flicks can. Instead, Vietnamese living in America tell their children ghost stories and share their memories of the monsoon rains and harvest festivals. I too store in my brain a million of those memories and myths, none of which have anything to do with America's involvement in the war, but that, as they say, is another story.

Vietnam-America. Whatever happened to that covetous embrace? America-Vietnam. What became of that illegitimate marriage?

Recently I read that a frail, crowded boat carrying refugees from Vietnam entered Malaysian waters with a peculiar sign hanging on its side. It read "USA remains on my boat." Bones, bags of GI bones. Missing remnants from that vicariously lost war, now found and carefully washed by impoverished Vietnamese hands and carried along as a treasure. They hope to bargain the bones for passage to the promised land.

"A set of GI bones is worth a whole family's tickets to the United States," so goes the gossip in Vietnam. Uncle Sam denies such handsome rewards, but Miss Saigon and her overabundant children dream on. Normalization with the United States is at hand, Americans will send aid, the trade embargo will be lifted, Hanoi is building an American embassy, American delegations are here to excavate oil fields in the Mekong Delta. There is a faint smell of that seductive dollar bill, the familiar scent of a GI's cologne.

I remember the Americans in Vietnam. While my father was an officer in the ARVN during the war, Americans were his allies, communists were his foes. Among the things we burned near the end of the war were self-incriminating photos of our American friends. One photo showed my father and his American advisers looking at a military map. There was a picture of my older brother standing next to the actor Robert Mitchum, who visited Vietnam to support the troops. Another photo showed Joanna, an American social worker, smiling sweetly next to my mother. Those pictures and many more went up in smoke to disclaim our haphazard and estranged friendship (although we later fled to America and became Americans).

"Your country didn't deserve all the shit from us," said the pool man at my parents' suburban home. A Vietnam vet, he wore a baseball cap with the word "Danang" on it. "I love your country, man," he continued. "I had a wonderful time there. If I had enough money I'd take a trip from Hanoi to Saigon." I once gave a dollar bill to another Vietnam vet who was panhandling in Berkeley. I told him I came from Vietnam. He threw the money back at me.

Sometimes I am asked how well Americans understand the Vietnam War. I don't know, I answer, but there is this wall in Washington. And you can sense its truth when you are there. All year long Americans come and leave poems and photos and flowers to those who died in Vietnam. Unlike all the memorials in America that depict past triumphs or happy endings, this dark wall stands alone and sacrosanct. If there are ghosts in America, they could comfortably congregate there, for it is the only American place of tragic consequences, this wall that over time has evolved in a tradition similar to that of a Vietnamese shrine.

My last memory of the Vietnam War: April 28, 1975, two days before Saigon fell to the advancing North Vietnamese Army. My family and I boarded the C-130 with other panicked refugees and fled. My father gave the American pilot a gift he had received from an American adviser years before: a silver gun encased in a hollow Bible. Two days later the war ended.

Vicky, a social worker who assists boat people in Hong Kong, traveled to the Mekong Delta to understand her clients' past. She encountered a boy who sat on a water buffalo amid a golden rice field. Instead of playing a traditional bamboo flute he had a boom box playing the songs of the Eurythmics. "What do you make of that?" Vicky asked.

"USA remains on my boat," answers the wooden sign. It tells more than it had intended to. And perhaps Stallone is right: Americans did indeed win the war. Vietnamese are ready to be Americans. Vietnamese want VCRs, democracy, Levi's jeans, freedom, Toyotas, happiness. The Vietnamese government offers the Cam Ranh Naval Base to welcome Uncle Sam again, if he ever wants to come back. Miss Saigon winks.

And me. Sometimes I go to a Vietnamese restaurant in San Francisco's Tenderloin District. I sit and stare at two wooden clocks hanging on the wall. The left one is carved in the shape of a florid S: the map of Vietnam. The one on the right is hewn in the shape of a deformed tooth: the map of America. Tick, tock, tick, tock. They run at different times. Tick, tock, tick, tock. I was born a Vietnamese. Tick, tock, tick, tock. I am reborn an American. Tick, tock, tick, tock. I am of one soul. Tick, tock, tick, tock. Two hearts.

Coming of Age in a Changing Nation

September 2000

The doe-eyed teenager in the internet cafe wept as she typed furiously into her computer that sultry morning in Saigon.

"What's the matter?" I asked.

Seventeen-year-old Nga Le, pretty and well-dressed, immediately turned and said she'd just had the most moving experience in her life and she was using the internet to tell some of her friends about it.

"I just saw *Boys Don't Cry*," she announced and, as she was saying this, her eyes brimmed again with tears. Le said she'd watched it twelve times and it left her devastated. "The saddest thing I ever, ever saw."

As with many Hollywood productions, a pirated video version of *Boys Don't Cry*, featuring Hillary Swank in her Oscar-winning performance of a young woman who posed as a man and was murdered, was available for a couple of dollars here in Saigon—or Ho Chi Minh City, if you like—long before the legal version appeared in US video stores.

Thanks to the information age, and people like Le, it quickly became one of the favorite films of the year in Vietnam.

Le can discuss what happened to Swank's character in detail, but don't ask her opinion about anything archaic like the Vietnam War or she'll immediately put on that bored look teenagers everywhere put on when confronted with a topic they know nothing about.

"The war?" she said. "Those fat American tourists come to look for signs of the war, but that has nothing to do with my generation. They're like archaeologists, digging up old things."

"Besides," she added with disdain, "that drama happened a long, long time ago."

Boys Don't Cry, on the other hand, only happened last night and, strange as it may sound, not being able to live one's true destiny is more profound to Vietnam's new population than any pithy observation about a war that now belongs to the history pages.

Here's something to consider: Vietnam's population since the war ended has more than doubled, going from thirty-five million in 1975 to eighty million at the turn of the millennium. Almost three out of four Vietnamese today have no direct memory of the Vietnam War.

Vietnam may have defeated America but these days her young are restless. They have their own modern drama to deal with, and it's called globalization, which has hit Vietnam like a hurricane.

They've replaced Uncle Ho's photos on their parents' walls with posters of Chow Yun Fat, *Baywatch* starlets, and the Backstreet Boys. They race motorcycles late at night down tree-lined boulevards, playing Rebels Without a Cause while the police look on helplessly. And they slip a video from Hollywood or Hong Kong into the VCR and marvel at the beauty and elegant possibilities that exist in the outside world.

Internet cafes have sprung up within the last few years in large cities and are crowded with young people surfing the web. Cell phones are cheaper than wired phones, and they are omnipresent. Dance clubs, record stores, shopping malls, video stores, and fashion and fitness magazines are the rage among those who can afford them.

So many changes so quickly have left a country full of young people going through an acute identity crisis—the reason, I suspect, why Le and a few others I interviewed found *Boys Don't Cry* so profound.

Though Vietnam remains a one-party-rule nation and claims a communist ideology, the government has since the early nineties eased its grip on the economy and ceased being a hard-core police state.

Indeed, after the collapse of the Soviet Union (Vietnam's main backer during the cold war), the ideology Ho Chi Minh once elevated to the level of religion fell quickly into the gutter. In order to save its own skin, the Communist Party rewrote its constitution to allow "private capitalism," and it reinstalled *doi moi* (a Vietnamese version of perestroika) to encourage economic reform.

As a result, the party's grip on society loosened considerably. Gone are the days when everyone had to report to local authorities for weekly Marx-Lenin indoctrination sessions. Gone are domestic travel permit requirements and the ration tickets, once issued by the state for citizens to buy rice and sugar from state-owned stores as a way to control people's movements and stomachs.

What followed is not exactly what Hanoi expected. The country now features a generation of young people who *di quay,* or "go wilding."

"The young are apolitical and materialistic," observed Chanh Nguyen, a chain-smoking poet and businessman in his late thirties, whose nervous demeanor may have to do with the conflicting nature of his two passions. Or perhaps, speaking so openly about Vietnam in a bar in Saigon, he was wary of eavesdroppers. "They grow up in a society where things are changing so quickly and so dramatically. Worse, there are no rules of law. All they see is everyone else struggling to make money. Materialism is really the only ideology that makes any sense to them."

The government blames Western influences for the growing juvenile delinquency and erosion of "traditional cultural values." But it is hardly free from guilt. Roughly half of the country's six thousand state-owned enterprises are inefficient, unprofitable, and losing jobs. The economy also suffers from widespread corruption, high corporate and personal income taxes, and a banking system that needs serious reform. Worse still, Vietnam long ago rescinded its socialistic commitments.

Resources for both education and health care dropped dramatically after the government adopted *doi moi.* The young are, as Chanh put it, "being dumbed down, blindsided with old rhetoric and a horrible education system."

Narrow, outdated syllabuses, overcrowded classrooms, and underqualified and underpaid teachers mean that students are not encouraged to develop their own ideas or to express them. Students are still required to memorize Marxist doctrines that have no application in the real world except for within the Communist Party.

Although Vietnam boasts the highest literacy rate in Southeast Asia—around 90 percent—the reality is that less than 38 percent go to secondary school, only about 9 percent attend college, and fewer than half of those graduate. And while urban areas have seen a rise in personal income, 25 percent of the country remains unemployed.

Duong Thu Huong, author of the internationally acclaimed *Paradise of the Blind*, a novel that examines and criticizes the errors of Vietnamese communism, once observed in a scathing essay widely read among Vietnamese living abroad that "Vietnamese youths are no longer idealistic. Today they are revolting as if to avenge the prior generations for their deceptions."

This new revolution comes with its own vocabulary:

di quay: to go wild, to get drunk, to stir up trouble;

song voi: to live fast, to hurry life and spend it away;

dua doi: to be competitive, to be greedy, to keep up with the Joneses;

van hoa toc do: speed culture; life that moves along at high speed.

For a few days in Ho Chi Minh City, Trang Huynh, 23, was my *Honda om*, my motorcycle driver. Huynh came up to the city from the Mekong Delta as a college student with a scholarship, but he soon gave up. He stood around five foot one and was conscious of his height. "I'm small because when I was growing up we didn't have enough to eat."

Now, in Vietnam's economic capital, he still struggled to make ends meet. "I couldn't continue schooling because even with a scholarship of around twenty-five dollars a month I was starving," he said. "I was head of my class, a math whiz, but what can you do with a degree in math? Teach? I'd starve as a teacher. Now, I have to do whatever I can to feed my family back home." On weekends Huynh moonlights as a wedding photographer.

His attitude—"to do whatever"—is a popular one, especially in urban areas. And often it results in an array of social ills.

The abortion rate, for example, is skyrocketing in Vietnam. According to the UN Population Fund, 40 percent of all pregnancies in Vietnam are terminated. With about 1.4 million abortions performed during the past year, the country has one of the highest abortion rates in the world. The local newspapers are full of reports of abandoned newborn babies and of the racketeers, including government officers, who sell unwanted children to foreigners, four hundred dollars for a girl, six hundred for a boy.

Drug problems are also increasing. Ecstasy is becoming common here, sold for two American dollars a pop, and the Vietnamese government estimates the number of heroin addicts at around one hundred thousand, although many social workers think it's a lot higher. Smuggled from China via the Golden Triangle, heroin long ago replaced the less harmful opium. In addition, shared needles are contributing to the spread of AIDS.

To further exacerbate the situation, Vietnam is home to a booming sex industry. A government report says more than one third of the country's service-related properties are engaged in the sex trade. A National Committee for AIDS Prevention survey conducted in the Mekong Delta region last year found that one in five prostitutes is infected with HIV.

Vietnam, in recent years, has also become famous for exporting its women. That is, many young women have sold themselves abroad to help their impoverished families, most from rural areas. Taiwanese and South Korean men flock to Vietnam on a regular basis under the pretext of looking for brides—paying anywhere between five thousand and fifteen thousand dollars for one—but many Vietnamese women actually end up not as wives but as prostitutes in brothels overseas.

Hieu Nguyen, 24, is one of Vietnam's brightest stars. Having attended college and learned English when he was eleven, Hieu, a handsome young man, speaks English fluently. A book translator and an editor for *Vietnam News,* an English-language newspaper in Hanoi, Nguyen makes almost six hundred American dollars a month in a country where the average income is around four hundred dollars a year. Yet he is timid about political criticism since all newspapers are under government control. When asked, however,

Nguyen reluctantly agreed that there were problems caused by state corruption and an inefficient bureaucracy.

"Our education system must improve if Vietnam's going to catch up with Thailand and Malaysia in the high-tech game," he said. "Vietnam is at a crossroad." Asked to specify, Nguyen politely refused. "I don't want to touch politics," he said apologetically and offered a dimpled smile.

Nguyen confessed to a private fantasy that's actually shared by many: he dreams of taking his wife to the United States to work and live someday. "I have friends making a lot of money over there. I would love to be in the States."

Trang Huynh, the motorcycle driver, on the other hand, has no dream at all. He makes about four dollars a day, eight dollars on a very good day. He said he is often depressed. Sometimes, when down, he races his motorcycle late at night with other *Honda oms*.

Trang and his friends flirt with death, going as fast as sixty miles per hour through empty city streets. Each pays around five dollars to race, with the winner taking all.

"Why take such risks?" I asked.

"Why not?" he laughed. "Who cares if we live or die?"

Nevertheless, Vietnam is a country at peace, and there's even a growing, albeit small, middle class. There's no discernible foreign enemy to stir the old nationalistic impulse. What's new, what's so unprecedented in Vietnam, is unfettered materialism and unprecedented individualism, the combination of which has dramatically altered if not already torn a hole in the age-old Confucian-bound social fabric.

But despite the enormous changes, despite all the new freedoms the young people boast about enjoying for the first time in their otherwise restricted lives, freedom of speech is not one of them.

They are free to get drunk, free to stay out all night, free to fornicate, to race motorcycles, to drop out of school, to do drugs, but they are not free to think critically for themselves. They are not free to tell their stories in any constructive way. There is no public forum, no space on the government-controlled opinion page for them to fully express their feelings.

Few young people I talked to had ever heard the terms "multi-party system" and "civil disobedience." All they know is that there is injustice and corruption and that they are helpless, lacking the creative and political language to describe their condition. And so, muted, they go wilding instead.

"Vietnam is a society where you can do anything you want as long as you don't write or draw or speak publicly about it," said The Tran of Hanoi, an antiques dealer and co-owner of a small hotel. "This is the hypocrisy that hasn't been overcome."

Yet while the authorities keep the Vietnamese people politically silenced, Vietnam's doors are open wide to the world. A rich person, for instance, can put up a satellite dish on his roof and catch CNN, MTV, BBC, and other Western sources of information. While bookstores and newspapers are governmentally controlled, fashion magazines and video stores are not.

The privately owned video stores are free to rent everything from Hong Kong kung fu movies and soap operas to Japanese animations to Hollywood films. A few even carry illegal but highly popular pornography starring blond Europeans and Americans.

These days old men—ministers and politburo members and ex-generals and city mayors—appear nightly on TV to warn the populace about the danger of "peaceful evolution" and harmful foreign influences. But they are preaching to deaf ears. Viewers can now change the channel or watch a video. The Communist Party continues to emphasize the finer points of collective strength, invoking memories of a war against invaders, but the young people of Vietnam, who, of course, do not share those ancient memories, have moved away from a parochial us-versus-them mentality.

Tinh Tran is a precocious fourteen-year-old in Hanoi. "If the ministers tell us to be 'vigilant against foreign influences,' then why are they sending their kids to school in the US and driving Lexus and Mercedes-Benz?" he asked. His favorite pastime is playing video games, but he captured the hypocrisy of the situation with uncanny cynicism. "They tell us to be good communists in school, but they live in big villas and their wives shop in Japan and Europe. They stink. They make no sense whatsoever."

The wall in the living room of Tinh's home tells a fascinating story. At the bottom is a nineteen-inch television set and a VCR. On top of the TV is a wooden family altar where photos of relatives who died fighting the French and Americans hide behind an urn of burning incense. Above that altar is a conspicuous white rectangle imprinted on the green wall. It is where, so I'm told, Ho Chi Minh's picture had hung for decades.

As a frequent visitor to Vietnam, I find it intriguing that in Vietnam there exist two distinct and contradicting realities, side by side. Red banners that hang between tamarind trees along boulevards still glorify the war against the foreign imperial powers and idolize Ho Chi Minh's greatness. Yet, close by are glaring billboards hawking Coca-Cola and Tiger Beers and Toyota. Noisy public speakers mounted on telephone polls that mouth off communist propaganda each morning are being drowned out by singers in karaoke bars and privately owned stereos that blast the likes of Britney Spears and Ricky Martin.

There's no competition, of course, in this chaotic shouting match. Hands down, the vision that is far more seductive and enticing comes from the colorful billboards, the TVs showing foreign films, and the sexy voices of Western pop singers on the stereo.

Indeed, for many of today's youths who are acquainted with Western pop music and cyber cafes and Hollywood movies, the Party—once the symbol of the struggle for independence and unification—is now a dinosaur whose propaganda rings hollow, if not irritatingly hypocritical and nonsensical.

Repeatedly, many young people I talked to said that the only time they felt proud of being Vietnamese was when Vietnam beat Thailand in a soccer match last year. Trang Huynh said that he "waved the flag for the first time in a long time. But only because of the soccer team, not because of the stupid government."

And Nga Le, too, lit up when the soccer game was mentioned. "I hope we win again. I've never seen so many people so happy at one time," she said. "You know, we have so little to be proud of."

These days, Ho Chi Minh's most famous slogan, "Nothing is more precious than independence and freedom"—once intended to spur his followers to sacrifice their lives in the bloody struggle to liberate Vietnam from the French and then the Americans—has been turned on its head with two words added on by the public after the cold war melted: "Nothing is more precious than independence and freedom—for yourself." In essence, Vietnamese youth want to pursue *their own* happiness, what Ho Chi Minh conveniently omitted when he adapted the American Declaration of Independence for his own use more than half a century ago.

What do the young people here want?

"A job" is often the reply. Preferably with a foreign company, for that means a high status among one's peers. Girls dress up in red *ao dai* dresses to vend foreign cigarettes and beers, and boys in white shirts and ties bow to potential customers as they sell high-tech goods from Sanyo and Sony. Anything from overseas is perceived as better, a step up the material ladder. Ultimately, their dream vacation, their dream destination, is California.

Vietnam is a country that's wholly unprepared for the forces of change, especially when those forces threaten to melt borders and challenge national identities. Since the war ended, Vietnam's story of itself has gone from one of pride to ignominy—once a country of citizens who defeated American imperialists at the height of the cold war, there is now the poor, confused, subservient man lurking at the edge of the global village, willing to make Nike shoes for two dollars a day. Red capitalism is now raging under communist flint skin.

Duong Thu Huong, that sadly unread novelist in Vietnam, is right. The young of Vietnam are, in a way, rebelling. But their revolution lacks any coherent direction. Collective malaise and mass desires for material wealth do not a movement make. While youth movements in Vietnam in previous generations changed the political direction of the country—the August Revolution in 1945 comes to mind, when youths responded to Ho Chi Minh's call and joined the fight against French colonialism—it is doubtful that this generation can do more than posture à la James Dean in *Rebel Without a Cause*.

For the last leg of my journey I spent a few rainy days in Hue, the imperial city where kings of millennia past lie sleeping in quiet tombs scattered along the Perfume River. In contrast, the royal pavilion near the city's center teems with foreign tourists who play kings and queens for an afternoon.

These camcorder-toting visitors from France and England and the United States pay handsomely to dress up as royalty in colorful silk brocades as they sit on throne-like seats while Vietnamese waiters in traditional dress serve them a royal dinner.

The scene on the ancient pavilion of Hue was a bit painful to watch. Yet it provided useful insights to this country. It pantomimed what life must have been like during the years that followed the first French gunship that sailed up the Perfume River and took over first the imperial city, then eventually the country, thus beginning France's brutal period of colonization, which was followed by several generations of Vietnamese rebellions and wars for independence.

Indeed, for almost a hundred years Vietnamese dreamed that their country would someday be free from foreign domination, and countless lives have been sacrificed toward that end. Finally Vietnam is at peace. Yet it occurred to me as I watched that young kowtowing Vietnamese who was bringing the middle-aged tourist a Coca-Cola on a lacquer tray that the old dream may never be realized. The waiter was not merely reenacting the distant past. Not exactly. More likely, he was prophesying Vietnam's retro-future.

Trash

June 1990

Last week I took a distant relative, newly arrived from Vietnam, on a tour of the UC Berkeley campus, where I once studied. He had been in awe of San Francisco's skyscrapers, and he stared with equal wonder at the stately halls and gates of my alma mater and at the hills dotted with large homes and villas. But when we walked past a large garbage bin filled with papers and carton boxes, he paused. Pointing to the heap of trash next to the architecture building he exclaimed with a shocked look on his face, "Brother, in Vietnam this stuff is all money!"

I, of course, know this. But in America how easy it is to forget. What I throw away today would have astounded me years ago.

This young man is not an environmentalist; he understands little about the world's ecology or the greenhouse effect. His comment simply reflects his own third-world background. He is, therefore, frugal and practical. What's more, he has a great respect for the materials we Americans discard as refuse, as waste. His family in Vietnam could live for a week recycling these papers, he tells me, and it pains him to see so much wasted.

"I can't believe you throw this stuff away," he shakes his head as we walk away from the pile of "trash," and I feel a slight tug of guilt—my garbage is filled with junk mail, newspapers, empty bottles, leftovers, things he would have recycled for cash.

At my parents' home my extended family recently gathered over a letter sent from a great aunt living in Danang. The letter itself is thin and sallow. Recycled for who knows how many times, the dark material reflects the poverty of the country from which it came.

"The poor country is condemned," observed one uncle haughtily. He drives a midnight-blue Mercedes-Benz.

Is it a sure sign, then, of a third-world immigrant's successful assimilation into an overdeveloped society when he can cast a snobbish glance back toward the impoverished world he left behind? We sit and ponder as to how we ever managed to live in that malaria-infested place where the sewer turns the river black as night. The green bottle flies the size of your toe, the unpaved road with potholes, the unbearable heat, the stench—didn't it all seem like a bad dream, my dear?

One cousin came back from two weeks of frolicking in Vietnam complaining of bad hotels. They have no streetlights in some parts of town, he says. They still wrap food in newspapers, and many people still smoke hand-rolled, filterless cigarettes. To the pedicab driver who was once an ARVN officer my cousin gave a twenty dollar bill. It's equivalent, you know, to that old man's monthly wage, he says.

As he tells his stories, I remember one night a few decades ago when these same relatives of mine took a carton full of expired food from a garbage bin by an empty supermarket. We had just arrived in America then. It was a day or so after Thanksgiving. We had been watching what the supermarket threw away each night and we marveled at the waste.

I was with them when we were stopped by two policemen. Indignant, my uncle-in-law, who was a former captain of the South Vietnamese Army, offered to return the food to its trash bin. But the officers, looking at our hungry faces, our shoddy clothes, shook their heads and demurred. "Help yourself," one of them said and they walked away.

I look back now to my homeland, to my yokel self, and admit how much I and the others, who left Vietnam so long ago, have forgotten. It is as if along with the pile of papers and uneaten food we have carelessly tossed away our memories. In our material success in America we have forgotten what it was that sustained us: our attachment to the land, our old identity.

If we were once shocked by America's opulence, we have long since learned to take it for granted that, well, there's plenty more where that came from.

Sure, we recycle at our convenience these days but we don't pause long enough to think about where anything comes from. We live in a fast-paced world. We have become consumers. We consume.

At home, after our excursion to the campus, my cousin helped me prepare dinner. A few pieces of apple and pear accidentally fell from my chopping block onto the floor. Immediately he stooped to pick them up. "Oh, don't do that," I wanted to say, but something in his meticulous gesture stopped me.

Instead, as I watched him, his bent back, his bare feet, a distant and long-cherished memory emerged. I am six years old standing at the edge of a golden rice field at harvest time in the Mekong Delta where my father came from, holding onto my grandmother's hand and watching farmers stoop to gather rice.

I had wanted to show my cousin America's grandeur, but it was he who showed me something sublime. There, on the shiny tile floor of my kitchen, my cousin, too, was busy gathering bits of our old identities, scattered pieces of our soul.

Accent

October 1999

Uncle Tho, my father's older brother, was a studious man. He arrived in America from Vietnam at the age of forty-four but nevertheless struggled to reeducate himself. He went to school nightly, got a BA, and then, through Herculean effort, graduated from law school. But that was when things started to fall apart for him.

Uncle Tho's accent was so thick that none of his interviews proved fruitful. No one wanted to hire him, not even as a paralegal. After a dozen or so interviews he gave up. "Listen, get rid of any slight suggestion of an accent," he would tell me bitterly. "Americans turn a deaf ear to foreign accents. You'll never get anywhere fast if you sound like a foreigner."

I already knew as much. Although I was eleven when I came here and am now comfortable with the language, whenever I get nervous, my accent thickens. It's as if I am back in my seventh-grade English class and forced to read a passage from some book out loud. I can still hear the snickering from my classmates as I stumbled over difficult passages, not understanding a word.

So I practiced and practiced and practiced. Every morning in the shower as I got ready for school I would open my mouth and enunciate certain words learned the day before, listening to their vibrations against the tile. "Business," I would pronounce. "Stress!" I would shout. "Necessary!" I could almost see the words with their sharp edges and round arches taking shape in the steamy air. I would try my best to rule over them.

But I also knew that it was far harder to bend one's tongue to accommodate the American ear than to assimilate. My uncle, for instance, was not rejected for lacking qualifications or intelligence. It was his unruly tongue that gave his foreignness away, pronouncing him interminably alien and, unfortunately, unemployable.

Uncle Tho never found a satisfying job. After a while, he resorted to working in his wife's grocery store in the Mission District in San Francisco and smoked and drank himself to death. He had believed in the American Dream, but its golden door was shut on him at the last minute. On his deathbed, ravaged by throat cancer, Uncle Tho whispered inaudible words and gasped for air.

It's been more than a decade now since he passed away, but I think of him sometimes at cocktail parties or conferences. I try to enunciate my words carefully, masking my foreignness with my Californian accent. In the back of my mind, I hear Uncle's warnings: "Speak like Connie Chung and you're okay. Talk like me and you end up running a grocery store."

The other day I took a friend to a Chinese restaurant in San Francisco and the waiter, newly arrived from Hong Kong, told us to "take the table to the night," having failed to pronounce the R in the word "right."

"Sure," my friend snickered, "and we'll probably stay 'til morning."

A funny retort, surely, but it reminded me of Uncle Tho on his deathbed and I was suddenly overwhelmed by an intense sadness.

"Cindy," I whispered to her, "listen, I have something to tell you."

"Yeah?" she said as she leaned over and combed back her golden hair, ready to hear me divulge my secrets.

But I had nothing say. Instead I did something that left us both in shock. I leaned over, stuck out my tongue, and swiftly licked her ear.

Viet Kieu
December 2000

We return in order to take leave. The boat person turned entrepreneur builds a nest in her hometown but then keeps traveling around the world, her passport as thick as a novel. The fake doctor plays sophisticated prodigal son in his mother's house for a few weeks before going back to who knows what menial labor in America. Others come back to stay for a year or two, but they stay as foreigners and they create an expat community, where they feel more comfortable among each other and not with the people they long ago left behind.

And some return only in their mind.

"It is easy now to return, but impossible to go home," one elegantly dressed forty-something Vietnamese expat from Paris told me one evening as we sat together and drank a light and fruity Beaujolais in a Saigon bar.

I myself have been back to a country that was once my home but is no longer. The country I remember and still yearn for is not the country I visit. Still, like a weaning addict, I go back, from time to time, to look and measure my losses, and, slowly, in my own way, to let go.

Over lunch in a restaurant in District I, Trang Huynh, my twenty-three-year-old *Honda om*—motorcycle taxi driver—rattles off to me the categories of Viet Kieu, or Vietnamese nationals living abroad. Of Viet Kieus, there are, he said, at least four.

Viet kieu dom: fake Viet Kieus. "There are plenty in Saigon now who dress up and pretend to be returning Vietnamese Americans to either cheat people out of their money or seduce young women.

This one story I know, well, this guy pretended to be a Vietnamese American from California. He spent good money and wined and dined this woman who owned this restaurant. They went on vacation together using her motorcycle, and he offered her a drink, and she woke up in the hotel without her money, watch, rings, and her prize possession, the Honda Dream II motorcycle."

Viet kieu moi di da ve: those who recently left and have already returned. "These people have not yet absorbed the refineries of the West but they want to show off their new wealth and status. They come home and look and act like peasants in nice clothes."

Viet kieu chinh cong: the real Viet Kieu. "Elegant, worldly— someone like you, Brother. They don't show off. They have more money than those who show off but they're quiet and you can only tell they're Viet Kieu because they give themselves away when they say thank you when the waiter brings them a drink of water. Local Vietnamese don't say thank you to waiters. We never ever say thank you."

Viet kieu yeu nuoc: patriotic Vietnamese expats. "It's what the government calls all returning Vietnamese from abroad—essentially giving a theme to those who return, no matter what their reasons may be. In my honest opinion, Brother, these people don't exist. If they really are patriotic, why would they escape in the first place? I myself wouldn't fit in this category had I left and come back. I am not patriotic and I haven't even left."

I do not necessarily share Trang Huynh's assessments, but I trust his earnestness. Besides, I have met one Viet Kieu in Saigon who belonged more or less to the second category.

One day while staying at a friend's house in the city's outskirts, a young woman named Lan came knocking. A few houses down another Viet Kieu had also turned up, she told me. His name was Quang. He was from California. And he told his mother's servant that he was bored. Lan, the doe-eyed teenage servant, asked if I would "keep Uncle Quang occupied."

"He's too smart and worldly," she said proudly. "He couldn't talk to anyone in the neighborhood."

So I obliged and went to visit him. Hanging on the wall of the living room of his mother's house were Quang's diploma from Harvard and a picture of Quang shaking hands with President

Clinton. There was a commotion in the back of the house, the sound of rain, and a green plastic bead curtain was lifted to reveal a slightly overweight man in a three-piece beige linen suit. He wore a glossy silk off-pink shirt, and from his breast pocket bloomed a purple handkerchief. The air was humid and already sweat ran down his temples. We shook hands and his palm felt wet and slippery.

I was impolite. I stared. The man before me resembled a Vietnamese W. C. Fields, albeit without a walking stick and pocket watch. I squinted a little and tried to imagine him in a black-and-white photo. No one I knew had worn a suit like that in years, and certainly not here in a city where most people still wear pajamas in the house and, more often than not, outside of the house. Something of the man was reminiscent of an Indochina past—the suit and handkerchief were the kinds of things my fourth great uncle would wear on Sunday to go downtown to meet his friends in Saigon when I was a child. But Fourth Great Uncle, who fought in World War I for the French in Verdun and lived for some time in Paris as a French citizen, was the last of his breed and died very old when I was seven or eight. Since his funeral I hadn't seen a suit like that, except perhaps in faded photographs of Ngo Dinh Diem, the South Vietnamese president who was murdered in a military coup the year I was born.

Quang affected a style that existed neither in America nor in Vietnam, if it ever existed at all. In any case, his courtliness was only an approximation of a distant past and, with the purple handkerchief, it seemed to border on parody.

From time to time his mother in black pajamas peeked out from behind the curtain of plastic beads. No doubt she must have thought that the way I was dressed—in jeans, a T-shirt, and Birkenstock sandals—meant her son's new guest was far beneath her son's social class in America.

The conversation was a dud. Quang sat stiffly, didn't say much, and his English was atrocious. He could barely speak English at all. When I offered that I went to Berkeley and then asked him about his PhD thesis at Harvard, his face turned ashen. He was genuinely surprised that I would notice the big diploma hanging on the wall behind him like the blade of a guillotine, and he seemed a little offended at my question. "Engineering thesis," he said and that was all.

I asked why was he shaking hands with Clinton. Quang brightened up. "Oh, I give money to him. Lots of money." I assumed he meant to Clinton's presidential campaign. "Yes," he nodded. "A lot of money."

Lan brought out tea and smiled appreciatively at me. She did not see that Quang was shooting daggers at her with his eyes. It occurred to me then that this was possibly her idea entirely, her stroke of genius, as it were. Quang, I thought, may never forgive her for this.

"Brother," Quang said, in Vietnamese, "how long have you been in America?"

"Since 1975. And you?"

Quang hesitated. His mother and servant were eavesdropping. "I came over in '87," he admitted.

"Oh," I said. "Quite impressive." He had received his PhD in 1990.

Among Vietnamese in America, there existed a strange unwritten caste system. Those who came early like me are seen as privileged and lucky—we belonged to the first wave, we didn't suffer under communist hands, and we were mostly educated, upper-class people who hadn't escaped on dingy, crowded boats; we avoided, that is to say, the bulk of the horror. Those who escaped later are seen as wretched, having been robbed of education back home and having suffered at the cruel hands of the communist government. Once in America they had to struggle twice as hard to keep up with the already established first-wavers. There had been countless stories of how many had gone into debt or become petty criminals in order to buy that much-coveted BMW or a gold Rolex.

I looked at the photograph again. Close up Clinton seemed to hover over Quang, the superachieving Viet Kieu. Their bodies seemed oddly disproportional to one another—a shoddy touch-up piece of computer graphic. Besides, the president's eyes were focusing elsewhere.

A troubling narrative thus unfolded quickly before me. Among those who haven't left Vietnam, there's a yearning to be somebody in America, so much so that a new mythology is woven into the modern Vietnamese imagination. If you leave, it says, if you escape to America, you'll come back Somebody. Vietnamese believe in it so strongly that many risked death at the hands of Thai pirates and drowning at sea in the eighties in order to reach the promised land. How many Vietnamese mothers sold all their jewelry, down to their wedding rings, in order to buy passage for their children to escape? How many died trying?

Those who did make it to America like Quang cannot bring themselves back to Vietnam without a sense of materialistic accomplishment, of golden transformation, as it were, even if in America none has actually been had. Returning, they feel obligated to give in to the myth and play a larger-than-life role.

I sipped my tea hurriedly, and it burned my tongue. I shifted uncomfortably in my chair. I had to get out. Stay and I might ruin a fantasy the man obviously went through some pains to construct. He had, besides, only a few weeks to live out this fantasy before going back to the States.

More sounds of rain—his gray-haired mother still peeked from behind the swaying green plastic beads, beaming with pride and expectation.

After a few more minutes I found some excuse or another to leave. I offered half-heartedly to come back the next day. Quang looked relieved, although he said, "You sure? Not want stay longer? Have lunch?" Then, just as quickly, he got up, brushed some imaginary dirt off of his immaculate pants, and walked me to the door.

"So long," he said at the gate, dabbing the handkerchief to his temple. "Thank you very much for coming. Yes. See you around."

You might have seen her.

She's the Vietnamese woman with high cheekbones and a beauty mark on her chin on the cover of the *New York Times Magazine* some three years ago for a story about the Viet Kieus. She's wearing a black dress, lounging on a velour couch, holding a martini while looking at her partner, co-owner of Saigon's famous Q Bar, where anybody who is anybody eventually appears.

Or you might have seen her photograph in the book *Passage to Vietnam*, wearing a bra and sunglasses astride her silver Vespa, holding a live chicken by its neck—a picture that made her forever infamous in Vietnam. Vietnamese who look at that picture will immediately recognize that she is not Vietnamese. Why? "No Vietnamese," offers an older woman at a bookstore in Saigon who stared at the picture frowning, "would ever hold a live chicken by its neck."

Phuong Anh Nguyen is an archetypal Viet Kieu—she left as a boat person with her family, suffered horribly on the high seas, remade herself in America, then returned a jet-setting cosmopolitan.

In the two decades since she left Vietnam, Phuong Anh, a beautiful, petite woman with a sad, sweet smile punctuated by a beauty mark above her lips, has been almost everywhere and done almost everything. You could find her on a kibbutz or at a wedding in Morocco, playing elephant polo in Nepal, trekking in Peru, or simply visiting close friends in San Francisco or New York or Paris.

Phuong Anh carries two cell phones, and she constantly has to add more pages to her passport. "I can't help it. If I have an opportunity to go somewhere, I will take it no matter what," she admits as she sits drinking at the posh, newly rebuilt Caravelle Hotel in Saigon. Q Bar is just across the street, but it is being renovated.

She counts in her immediate circle writers, lawyers, millionaires, chefs, hotel owners, artists, NGO workers, and even a few movie stars. Matt Dillon once flew in and for a few days she was his guide; Gary Trudeau devoted two weeks of "Doonesbury" to her story. She's been interviewed on CNN by Peter Arnett, attended Prince Sihanouk's coronation party in Phnom Penh, vacationed at writer William Shawcross's mansion outside London.

Don Johnson came by and left a note, "Sorry I missed you." She has dined with Norman Mailer, had drinks with Walter Cronkite, Norman Schwartzkopf, Gary Hart, Robert DeNiro, and JFK Jr. and Daryl Hannah. In fact, Hannah was wearing her famous Q Bar T-shirt when she got off the plane in New York with Kennedy, and when the photo showed up in *GQ* it started a fury of interest and even more exposure for her bar and restaurant. *Saveur, Annabel, National Geographic,* the *Asian Wall Street Journal,* and many other media outlets carried stories about Phuong Anh and her Q Bar.

Yet few know who she is. Hers is not a household name. She's not a model (she turns down offers); she's not an artist. "Oh God, no, I can't paint or write or take a good picture to save my life," she says, laughing.

She's an entrepreneur, it's true, but few entrepreneurs have such a mystique. No. What attracts so many people to this petite woman is a certain radiant inner strength. In fact, having known her for a decade, if I had to choose one word to describe her it would be "fearless."

One day a few years ago when we were eating oysters at a fancy restaurant in San Francisco, Phuong Anh suddenly blurted out, "You know, for years I couldn't eat oysters."

"Why not?" I asked, astonished. Ever since I had known her—since the mid-eighties—she'd always loved oysters.

"When we were on that island, all we had was oysters and coconuts and I thought I'd die if I had to eat another oyster."

That island—one of the thousand in Indonesia's archipelago—was deserted until her family and a hundred other Vietnamese boat people were shipwrecked there in 1979. On that island she buried her older sister, dead from injuries received when she was raped by Thai pirates, and an older brother who was murdered trying to save his sister.

Though we've been friends for a long time, I never ask her to tell more than what she is willing to divulge on her own. But I know this much: in America it took her family years to readjust—her mother suffered depression and mental breakdowns, her father fell into silence—but readjust they did. Two of her siblings settled and became dentists and another a real estate agent; but Phuong Anh grew restless and in 1991 went back to Vietnam with her then-boyfriend, the photographer David Jacobson, despite her parents' objection.

Among the first few to come home, she was single-handedly responsible for revitalizing Saigon's high-end pubs. She was defining Vietnam's sense of style. She paid meticulous attention to detail—every chair, every candleholder, every lamp was custom-designed to her liking. The mural had to be painted just so. The light had to be a certain tone at night, and the music selection had to be just right—setting a festive mood, but low enough for conversation in the early evening, and louder, with more excitement, as the evening wore on.

The result was that Q Bar became an instant hit. The rich and famous flocked to her bar. And Viet Kieus by the dozens gathered there at any given night to hang out with one another, a colony of expats comparing notes with each other about their new Vietnamese experience. And Phuong Anh, well, she was its reigning queen, a gregarious hostess.

And her clothes, well, her clothes—the bra as streetwear—are invariably copied by the wealthy and daring in Saigon. Her wardrobe also earned her a letter of reprimand by the communist committee.

But deep down, she once admitted to me, she returned to Vietnam to face her demons. She went to Vietnam the way she ate her first oyster in America, that is to say with gusto, chasing it down with cold vodka. Then the years wore on and eventually she let go of much, but not all, she says, of her rage.

A few years ago, at her mother's urging, to put her past in perspective she rented a boat and went searching for that island in Indonesia to retrieve her sister's remains. When she thought she had found the island, her sister's grave was gone, washed away. "There was nothing left," she says.

Today, sitting in her bar, she's a bit tired and weary. The building has been under renovation, but sometimes she's not sure she wants to reopen.

"Eight years, on and off, in Vietnam. I still have lots of my stuff in Europe and New York. Besides, I have so many other things to do," she says. Among her current projects: buying antiques in India for a friend, maybe writing a cookbook ("new, interesting dishes from Vietnamese all around the world"), investing in a Los Angeles restaurant, a New York hotel. But she hasn't given up Vietnam either. She sees potential here. She sees improvement. Slowly but surely, a growing middle class. And soon her bar will reopen with a restaurant to boot, featuring a chef flown in from Europe. "Vietnam even has MTV now," she says, laughing.

Where is home, then, I ask?

She sighs. She doesn't like the question. Her answer is as non-committal as it was when I first knew her: "Pasadena, I suppose, where my family is. But where do I want to live? I don't know.

Maybe New York. Maybe London. Maybe San Francisco. But I also belong here, in Vietnam."

This is, I think, her strategy. To have many homes. To belong to many places all at once. To keep traveling so she can have control over her past, to own it. Many Viet Kieus I know are like her. Born in Vietnam, remade elsewhere, the world suddenly shrinks to a village. Going back and forth becomes easy, seductive—they have turned into some of the first global villagers.

But Phuong Anh travels more than anyone I know. Almost compulsively. The world is, and please forgive the pun, her oyster now. She has friends on five continents and any given year she is likely to visit a third of them. If Phuong Anh ever stops moving, she tells me, "Who knows, a different person might emerge."

But not to worry. There's little chance of that. She's planning a New Year's Eve party for some close friends, around fifty of them, in Laos.

"We're all going to meet in Luang Prabang, Laos," she declares as she stares dreamily out to the street full of roaring motorcycles. "We're going to ride elephants in the jungle and take boat trips down the Mekong River and drink champagne. Andy, you've got to come."

In Dalat, a small city on a high plateau full of pine trees, waterfalls, and persistent morning fog, I am coaxed by an American television crew into revisiting my childhood home. The quaint pinkish villa on top of a hill is now abandoned, its garden overrun with elephant grass and wildflowers, its iron gate rusted, tilting to the side.

I hesitate. Do I want to go in? I am not given a choice. Someone breaks the door in the back. We go through the kitchen and, once inside, I try to recover myself.

Then, taking a deep breath, I proceed to explain my past to the camera. Here's the living room where I spent my childhood listening to my parents telling ghost stories, and there's the dining room where my brother and I played ping-pong on the dining table. Beyond is the sunroom where my father spent his early evenings listening to the BBC while sipping his Johnnie Walker whiskey and soda.

I go on like this for some time, until we reach my bedroom upstairs.

"Every morning I would wake up and open the window shutters to let the light in," I tell the camera excitedly as I proceed to do so. "Just like this. See?"

When my palm touches the wooden shutter, however, I suddenly stop talking. There is confusion among the film crew. I am no longer an American adult narrating his past. The sensation of the wood's rough, flaked-off paint against my skin feels exactly the same after three decades. Heavy and dampened by the weather, the shutter resists my initial exertion but, as before, it gives easily if you know where to push. And I do.

The shutter makes a little creaking noise as it swings open to let in the morning air—and with it a flood of unexpected memories.

I am a Vietnamese child again, preparing for school. I hear my mother's lilting voice calling from downstairs to hurry up. And I smell again that particular odor of burnt pinewood from the kitchen wafting in the cool air. Outside in my mother's garden, dawn lights up leaves and roses, and the world pulses with birdsongs. Morning dew on blades of grass. A self-contained world.

I remember too that sense of insularity, of being loved. It's a sentiment, I am sad to report, that has eluded me since my family and I fled our homeland in haste for a challenging life in America at the end of the war.

Living in California I had heard much about holistic healing and talk of long-forgotten emotions being stored in various parts of the body; but I had never truly believed that until this moment. Yet, it is hard for me to deny that there's another set of memories hidden in the body, and the way to it is not through language or even the act of imagination, but through the senses.

Now I know. I mean *really* know. There are memories, and there are *memories*. I once took pride in the belief that I remembered my Vietnamese childhood clearly. But what the mind forgets, the body might hold dear.

A long time ago my family and I had abandoned that lovely home on the hill of Dalat abruptly. In America I used to speak of the house with its rose garden and of a Vietnamese childhood that, despite the war, was a kind of fairy tale. I recalled Christmas in Dalat when we gathered pinecones and wild mushrooms. I remembered playing hide-and-seek with my friends among the trees and the hills nearby. I remembered singing at the top of my lungs and hearing my own echoes coming back through the woods. If there is a home that I am sentimental about in Vietnam, this is it.

In America I sometimes would dream of going into the house and taking shelter in it once more; at other times I would dream that nothing had changed, that the life I had left continued on without me and was waiting impatiently for my return. Then there were the nightmares in which I saw it as it was—empty and gutted—except that I was still a child abandoned within its walls. I would wake up in tears. I suppose, in my own way, I never ceased to mourn its loss.

But no more.

I re-enter a childhood home on a windblown hill one cloudy day with a television crew and emerge now with an unexpected gift—a fragment of my childhood left in an airy room upstairs.

I feel oddly blessed. Having touched once more the place where I used to live, I can finally say what I had always wanted to say after all these many years: good-bye.

On the outskirts of Hue the old woman with blackened enamel teeth—an old Vietnamese tradition of beauty—tells me she'd never crossed the Perfume River to see the imperial city of Vietnam. "Well, actually, I did once," she says, her eyes staring into the distance. "When I was a little girl I went to see the emperor on his throne. That must have been seventy years ago."

"But it's only two kilometers away," I say, a bit incredulous.

She shrugs. She looks toward her dirt-smeared great-grandchildren playing by the bamboo grove in the garden and the flock of chickens near the jasmine bush, as if to answer, "Whatever for?"

Even the celebration in the Imperial City to commemorate the end of the Vietnam War left the woman unmoved. "I've seen too many wars," she says dismissively.

And so, alas, have I. I lived here for a year, on and off, near the end of the war when my father was stationed with his soldiers in the Imperial City. Nine years old, I rode my bicycle with my older siblings across the river in the summertime, playing games in the empty chambers of an ancient palace where concubines once lived and where mandarins and kings wrote their poetry while gazing at the moon.

I remember drifting down the Perfume River in a bamboo boat some starry nights, my father telling stories about his visits to America and Europe and Japan, and me listening in my mother's arms. I remember my French-educated father's stories of snow. Snow on the gilded bridges across the Seine and in the well-groomed parks of Paris, snow across his bunker's window when he was a military exchange cadet in Denver, Colorado, and snow on barren trees and moss-covered rock gardens and the temple roof-tops of fabled Kyoto. I remember wishing for America with all my heart then, wishing for wings or for the boat to drift on downriver and away from the crazy war until we found ourselves under the Golden Gate Bridge. After hearing his stories, I remember standing on tiptoe on top of a chair next to our opened fridge, my hands in the freezer compartment scraping and scraping at the frost until my fingers were numb. Even then, with eyes closed and a modest snowball in my palm, I had begun to travel. Or was I trying to commune with my worldly father?

The old lady insists I come inside, and she offers me tea. So I park my bicycle and go into her little house and sit and regard the faces of her dead relatives staring out of faded photos on the top of the cabinet in the living room. The pictures are numerous, easily more than a dozen. "We go back five generations here," she says as she pours.

When I mention that I used to live in Hue too, and that my father was a commander in the region during the war, the woman exclaims that she remembers him. She is impressed. "Ah, a son of a general visiting my humble home," she says, giggling.

"I remember once seeing your father's motorcade going past. Dark skin," she says. "Very heroic-looking man." She asks how he is.

"He is fine," I answer. "Still healthy." I want to say, "But also sad." Sad because he lost the war.

I go back but he would not. Could not. I visit but he only dreams. I go now to Vietnam with the ease of someone for whom the borders are porous, but it is not the same with my father. Trang

Huynh, it seems, would have to invent another category for him: *viet kieu yeu nuoc khong ve:* those who are truly patriotic but who will never return as long as communism reigns—Viet Kieus who only dream of going home. My father could never allow himself the luxury of returning, even as he talks of Vietnam almost daily. He would not go back when his enemies are still here, still running the country. The wounds of defeat are still deep and unhealed. He longs for Vietnam but he remains forever an exile.

As for me, I travel constantly and Vietnam is but one of many destinations now. I got what I thought I'd wished for. It was here in Hue as a child, on the Perfume River, in the summer, with the lotus blooming, that I had dreamed of a larger world. Now a worldly traveler, I find myself envious of an old lady who wouldn't cross the river she could see from a distance.

The world is made up of those who move and those who do not, and increasingly it's populated by the former. But the old lady is not untouched by the exodus. One of her sons now lives in America. "He sends home money," she says proudly. "He's very successful. My son lives in Cali." Then she wonders out loud, "How big is this city called Cali, do you know?" I tell her it's California, and it's a state bigger than Vietnam, but this doesn't register. "My son in Cali is a very good son," she reiterates. "He sends money home every month."

The flies are buzzing between us as we regard one another across an old, tea-stained wooden table, but it might as well be an ocean between us. For her, crossing the nearby river is a journey, whereas for me Paris or Bangkok or New York is a matter of scheduling.

Wars are waged, generations come and go, the last emperor is long gone, yet the old lady stays in her little garden. I am, dear Granny, envious of the ease with which you feel connected to the tiny plot of land and with the dead and the past—whereas I, as in Thomas Wolfe's curse, cannot go home again.

I have been reshaped elsewhere. I have acquired many additional homelands. But I know this also: one who crosses the border suffers a certain disconnect. Or rather, I am rooted in numerous particu-larities, in several languages, but although the world is now at my beck and call and my friends and relatives are scattered in many countries, I feel often utterly alone.

That I can now visit Vietnam does not quench my thirst for Vietnam. I long for another country, the one I grew up in, the one in the distant past, accessible only in memories and dreams, where the borders were not yet crossed. But like it or not, the sentimental garden has long been trampled underfoot.

In any case, time to leave. The old lady sees me out. "Tell your parents I say hello. Wish them good health for me," she says. It's as if they've been friends all their lives.

As I get on my bicycle she turns her attention back to her little universe. She calls out to her chickens and tosses rice from her pajama pockets and they gather, clucking near her feet. Something in her gesture, with the smell of jasmine wafting in the air, makes me teary-eyed.

I ride away toward the river, which is running swift today. For some distance I can still hear her calling out for the chickens— "Here, chickadee, chickadee"—and her grandchildren's laughter reverberating from somewhere among the bamboo grove.

The scrawny street vendor in Hanoi studies my eyes, my lips.

"Brother," he says, "yours is not a Vietnamese face. It's a face that has not known suffering." Then he adds through a sigh, "Had I escaped to America, maybe I too would have such a face—a Viet Kieu face."

In Vietnam my face and body take on mythological proportions. When a cousin proudly introduces me to a friend, someone who has tried a dozen times in vain to escape, the man promptly reaches over to squeeze my thigh. I have no doubt that this is an impersonal gesture. Visions of double-tiered freeways and glassy high-rises are to be extracted out of the Viet Kieu's flesh. Squeeze a little harder and, who knows, you might just see Disneyland.

At a dinner party thrown in my honor by my relatives in Hanoi, people ask me to explain the intricacies of virtual reality, American foreign policy in the Middle East, and, while I'm at it, genetic engineering. They think my odd Americanized Vietnamese accent is perfectly charming. At another party my American passport is read like a comic book by my various relatives. As the entry and exit stamps of Greece, France, Mexico, Thailand, and a dozen other countries flutter past one cousin's eyes, she looks up at me and declares dreamily: "Cousin, such happiness! It's as if you have wings!"

Indeed, if in the last three thousand years or so it was generally understood that a Vietnamese soul is tied to home and hearth, in the last few decades a new idea has subverted the poetry of insularity: escape. In the decades that followed the end of the war, *vuot bien*—escape from Vietnam—has probably crossed every Vietnamese mind.

As it is, Vietnamese nationalism—that firebrand weapon that defeated the Chinese, Mongolians, French, and Americans—seems to have withered in its old age. While elderly Vietnamese leaders continue to emphasize the finer points of collective strength, citing memories of wars against invaders, the young of Vietnam have moved away from a parochial us-versus-them mentality. If Ho Chi Minh, the father of Vietnamese communism, once preached independence and freedom to his compatriots, today it's the Viet Kieu, those like me and my family, persecuted by Ho's followers and forced to escape overseas, who, upon return, exude freedom and independence.

As a Viet Kieu, I am often not just an individual but, to many, an icon against hopelessness, a character who took the high road and through whose life many can live vicariously. Familiarity and constant interactions over the last few years may have diminished the awe and glamour, but there is still an expectation here that a Viet Kieu, were he willing, could fulfill many an impoverished Vietnamese wish list.

I am, for example, mistaken on the streets of Vietnam for Santa Claus. One afternoon, a twelve-year-old street urchin named Tam nonchalantly asks if I might adopt him and send him to school. A young woman named Phuong, her face deformed by a skin disease, also begs for help; "Brother, you can perform a miracle: pay for my operation." And how many times, I wonder, have complete strangers—officials, rickshaw drivers, shop owners, ex–Viet Cong guerillas—offered me their daughters' hands in marriage?

In the old quarters of Hanoi, my aunt-in-law's neighbor, a young piano teacher, develops a crush on me. The aunt, who invited me to stay at her home, whispers, "Nephew, be careful."

That I had answered, "Yes, I do like Chopin," was clearly for the music teacher a declaration of romance. Chopin's "Polonaise" in various keys in due course echoed for hours from next door each afternoon, riding the humid air to my bedroom window.

In Vietnam as a child, I remember being moved by the national anthem that emphasized blood sacrifice to protect the sacred land. I remember feeling inspiration and awe staring at ripened rice fields at dusk. But that, as they say, was another life, a long time ago.

For me, as well as for many other Vietnamese of my generation, those birth ties were severed and our innocence died the day we crossed the ocean to distant shores.

Returning today, an odd gap appears between my countrymen and me. If I am some archetype in Vietnam's new narrative of itself—a modern-day Odysseus of sorts, someone that those who stayed imagine they can become if they were to flee overseas—I feel a stranger in my own homeland. Vietnam is an eighteen-hour flight from San Francisco, but it is also an impossible journey. The jet plane does and does not take me home again. Or rather, I go home again but the country of my childhood memories is long gone, replaced by a collective yearning of possibilities beyond the provincial.

In Vietnam there is a movie called *People's Love* made by a Vietnamese director about a Viet Kieu, the first film on the subject. It belongs to Trang Huynh's definition of the *viet kieu yeu nuoc*—the patriotic Viet Kieu. In the movie a Vietnamese American doctor, disillusioned with American life, returns home to find love and redemption. Such is the predictable sentimental script, funded by the state. It drew very few viewers.

I think the unfolding Vietnamese epic is closer to the reverse. Vietnam's innocence died with the birth of the Viet Kieu—the birth of the Vietnamese Diaspora. Vietnamese twenty-first-century romance is not with land, river, and rice field, but with glamour, with cosmopolitan and borderless life.

Still, I can no more deny my own sense of displacement in the new Vietnam than can I deny my role in the new Vietnamese imagination. No wings sprout from my back, but I have nonetheless brought a boon back to my own homeland: myself. I am evidence that the outside world exists.

The Dead Travel
August 2001

"'Til death do us part," that age-old marriage vow, has to Confucian ears always sounded a little, well, noncommittal. In Vietnam, death is not the end of relationships, it only deepens them.

A traditional Vietnamese worships his ancestors. He talks daily to ghosts. Every morning, every night, he lights incense and offers food and drinks to the spirit of his ancestors, prays for protection, and asks for advice. On special holidays he burns paper offerings so that his loved ones in the spirit world will have all the things they could possibly need. If someone claims to have seen his grandfather's ghost the night before, or if an ancestor long departed returns in his dream to give him advice, few would question whether or not it was true. More likely his neighbor would offer to decipher the meaning of the visitation.

If you travel along rural roads in my homeland, you will see rice fields full of old graves rising above the waterline. In the gardens of some houses, people are buried among patches of vegetables and bamboo groves where children play. Life and death coexist in close proximity in the Confucian cosmology—an intimate dance.

Though we have spent more than a quarter of a century now in California, my family is still trying, with various levels of success, to live out some of these Confucian ideals, especially when it comes to the business of burials. This was most evident when we buried my maternal grandparents in San Jose, California. Trouble was, my grandfather died and was buried in Saigon in 1971, at the height of the war, and my grandmother died in the late nineties at the age of ninety-eight in Silicon Valley.

Grandma's single wish was to be buried side by side with her beloved husband. When Grandfather died years ago, she bought a plot of land next to his grave in a cemetery in the center of Saigon called Mac Dinh Chi. On his tombstone she wrote a poem that, translated into English, goes something like this:

Suddenly the zither's string broke
and disrupted our sweetest harmony
yin and yang—apart in one stroke
'lone, alone, trills the nightingale
her bitter threnody.

As a child I had memorized this poem and could recite it on command. I remember it well because many a Sunday morning I would accompany Grandma and my mother to tend Grandpa's grave. There we would set new flowers in a vase, wash the marble tombstone, then light incense and burn paper offerings. I also remember helping Grandma weed the empty plot next to Grandpa's as she prepared it for her own final rest.

Unlike most couples in their generation my paternal grandparents' marriage was not arranged but a love match. It was evident in the volumes of poetry they wrote to each other during their years together. One of my fondest childhood memories is of sitting on the cool tiled balcony of their villa in the suburb of Saigon with my cousins and siblings during the Autumn Moon Festival. Grandpa and Grandma, in their silk brocades, would sit on their chairs and recite their favorite poems to one another as they drank tea. We grandchildren would listen and applaud the poetry-reciting couple.

Alas, Grandma's wish to be buried with her husband was interrupted when communist tanks rolled into Saigon four years after he died. Grandma was adamant about staying—"Who will attend your grandfather's grave if I leave?" she kept asking. In perhaps the most Confucian moment of their lives, my mother, uncles, aunts, and cousins all got down on their knees and begged her to come along. "How can we forgive ourselves if no one is left behind to take care of you?" they asked.

And so, Grandma's love of the living finally won out over her yearning for the dead. At the last hour, before the airport closed, she grabbed her purse and a few dresses and stuffed them in a plastic bag and came along with her children and grandchildren to America.

But the years here in California for my grandmother were years of longing and regret. She regretted leaving Vietnam, and she missed the Sunday rituals of tending to her husband's grave.

Exile for her had been a kind of tearing of the soul. Years ago, when she was still lucid, Grandma bought a wooden clock carved in the S shape of Vietnam from a Vietnamese store in Anaheim's Little Saigon. Above her bed the clock ticked mournfully, a constant reminder of how long she'd spent away from her home and hearth. Sometimes she would watch that clock tick as she counted her Buddhist rosary and then cried silent, bitter tears.

I remember once she asked me how far Vietnam was from California. I shrugged, "Well, I guess it's about eighteen hours." Hearing this, Grandma made a scowling face and snapped, "If our country is only less than a day away by your measurement, then tell me how come I've been waiting for fifteen years, seven months, and eight days now and I am still here in America?"

In America, Grandma no longer dreamed of Grandpa the way she did when she was living in Vietnam. As senility began to show, she often wondered aloud whether ghosts could cross the ocean and, if they could, why Grandpa hadn't visited her in her dreams. "Is the ocean too big?" she'd ask. "Has he gone to Nirvana? Has he forgotten me?"

When news arrived from relatives in Saigon that the communists were about to raze the famous cemetery in the center of town where Grandpa was buried, we hid it from her. Full of Southern elites, the cemetery was an eyesore to the Northern rulers who wished to erase all memories of the previous regime. Our entire clan pooled together a large sum of money and sent it to a cousin still living back home to have Grandpa's remains cremated and placed in a Buddhist temple.

When the cold war ended, we sent another cousin from California back to Vietnam. His mission: to bring Grandpa's ashes to the United States. His was a journey worthy of a postmodern movie, one in which he navigated red tape both in Vietnam and America, greasing palms along the way and fighting with the cousins back home who didn't want to let Grandpa's remains go abroad. But he succeeded. In a Vietnamese Buddhist temple near Sacramento, California, Grandpa's urn waited for my grandmother to live out the rest of her days.

My grandmother finally passed away early last year, and their two urns sat on a Buddhist altar amidst wafting incense smoke and banging gongs and chanting monks in San Jose. Then, at the cemetery, her children and grandchildren all got down to our knees and bowed to our grandparents before we buried them both together.

I remember the whole clan wore white headbands. We wept and prayed and lit incense and burned paper offerings. But inwardly we were also glad. The dead were now together at last, and at least, despite enormous changes in our own lives, some promises could still be kept: the living had performed their filial piety duties, even if it took navigating across borders and an ocean.

And, I hope, Grandma's nightingale can now sing a happier tune.

Christmas in Dalat, Christmas in San Francisco

December 1993

Wild orchids and painted pinecones—these things I remember of Christmas in Vietnam. It was in Dalat, the mountain city with its persistent fog and whispering evergreens, that I first celebrated Christmas. My father had been transferred there after the 1968 Tet Offensive, and he'd taken the entire family with him.

The distant bombing and the tropical heat of Sadec in the Mekong Delta were replaced by Dalat's cool, fresh breezes and romantic lakes. I was five years old, a child running free on fallen pine needles and tall green grass as I searched for wild mushrooms, pinecones, and orchids for Christmas decorations. My brother, sister, and I would each carry a wicker basket and eventually fill them with all that nature had to offer. Those days, we never bought Christmas decorations.

We used to sing. And by singing I mean spontaneously. As children we were not at all self-conscious, and we sang with gusto although often off-key. In the woods, early in the morning, we sang carols and chased each other, and sometimes the neighborhood kids would join in. Afterward our sweaters and hair would be embedded with pollen and pine needles. A sparse town then, our laughter and singing echoed and resonated among the brooks and streams.

At home we helped our mother decorate the tree. Its fresh fragrance brought the outdoors inside with us. My mother would roll cotton into the shapes of little chicks and angels with wings and she'd place them on the branches. The cones and mushrooms we painted green and red and blue and hung them everywhere in the living room. These ornaments were all the decoration we needed.

When my paternal grandmother came downstairs all dressed up in her *ao dai* dress, she would take us to Mass. She held my hand and led me and my siblings on the dirt road to a local church whose bells clamored and rang out in the air. Though I wasn't a Catholic, I remember feeling a spiritual devotion in that church. Everyone was smartly dressed and smiling. People sang and read their psalms. Afterward the priest distributed candy for the children. I remember it was early evening, the sun had sunk behind a bank of fog as we walked home, and the world was glowing in a lavender hue.

Before going home we would stop by the Hoa Binh market to buy some fruits and baguettes. Children with pink round cheeks held their mothers' hands and young adults in their best clothes walked around to show off their attire. The strawberries and plums we would eat on the way home.

At home, the best part of the Christmas dinner was dessert. My mother, a consummate baker, would make the traditional *buche de Noel,* a chocolate-covered cake in the shape of a log with a tiny Santa Claus sitting on top. Then my father would open the champagne and pour each of us a glass. We didn't receive any gifts as children did in America, but we didn't need any and never felt the loss.

Those are my favorite memories of Christmas in Vietnam. If you think such memories are out of place in a country whose image is made of conical-hatted figures working in rice fields, then you haven't been to Dalat. Dalat, built by the French as a hill station resort, was for the most part a peaceful town, until near the end of the war. For those of us who had the fortune to live there, the war was often at a distance; unlike the popular American belief shaped by Hollywood films, Vietnamese did not always live under constant terror and in half-burned villages. Instead, what we had in Dalat was a gentle small-town life that I haven't found again living here in America.

These days our Christmas is a big fanfare in the San Francisco Bay Area. My paternal grandmother is long gone but the Christmas trees are heavy with trinkets and baubles at my siblings' houses.

We vie to show off to one another how well we decorate our homes: Santa on the roof, reindeer on the lawn. We beg to be the one to serve dinner on Christmas Eve, and the meal is often replete with seafood and my father's favorite dish, bouillabaisse, and, of course, roasted turkey and wine and champagne. It is a testimony, I suppose, to how well we fare in the land of plenty.

So many years have passed since the war ended, yet it is not the horrors of war that dwell now in my mind during Christmastime. It's the transcending peace in a tranquil world that is now lost. Dalat, too, like the rest of Vietnam, is crowded with people, and the forests are thin. Even the weather had changed, growing hotter with fewer trees.

Still, I bet there are children running and laughing as before, there among the pine needles and singing brooks on that high plateau I once called home.

Two Passports
August 2001

Two passports—one new, the other old—arrived yesterday. The new, with its tough blue cover and pristine, rigid pages that still resist my prying fingers, is a stark contrast to the ink-stained, mud-smeared epic next to it, now punctured and rendered obsolete. In the old passport I am a young man looking out to customs officers everywhere with a kind of trusting optimism. The skin that glows, the red lips, the dark wavy hair that draped over my brows all convey something of innocence—a young man on a quest.

In the new passport the photo shows someone else entirely: a weathered man approaching middle age with a sad smile and fine wrinkles around his eyes and, worse, a receding hairline. I look at this photo—myself in the present—and wonder where did the time go? Every man is vain and I, of course, am no exception. In my late twenties I was often mistaken for a college student instead of a guest lecturer. And it was only a few years ago that a new intern at my news service mistook me for a fellow intern and not her editor. Then—who knows when exactly?—the wrinkles came and the hair fell and fell and fell.

In search of meanings and solace, I flip through the old passport. The entry and exit stamps from various countries flutter out and hang in the ether like musical notes from some nostalgic rhapsody: France, I'm in my lover's arms in an attic in winter, looking out to the Seine where snow is falling on a gilded bridge; Vietnam, I'm sailing down the river toward the perfumed pagoda amidst limestone mountains while white cranes fly overhead; Mexico, my best friend and I are eating conch and drinking margaritas on a white sandy beach, the Atlantic Ocean lapping at our bare feet; Nepal, I'm sleeping near the world's rooftop with the roundest and brightest moon I've ever seen hanging out my window and turning the top of Mt. Everest into a glorious blue dome.

A parade of beatific moments comes flooding back and gives me courage to look at the photo in the new passport once again. I now see that it's not a sad smile. It's a knowing smile. After all, mine is what it should be: a traveler's face.

About the Author

Andrew Lam is an award-winning syndicated writer, an editor with the New American Media, and a former commentator on National Public Radio's *All Things Considered*. He co-founded New California Media and his essays have appeared in dozens of newspapers and magazines across the country, including the *New York Times,* the *Los Angeles Times,* the *San Francisco Chronicle,* the *Baltimore Sun,* the *Atlanta Journal,* the *Chicago Sun Tribune, Mother Jones, The Nation,* and *Earth Island Journal. East Eats West,* a companion to this volume, was published in 2010 by Heyday.

Related titles from Heyday

East Eats West: Writing in Two Hemispheres
Andrew Lam
"Alarmed and delighted, I voraciously read *East Eats West.*"
—Maxine Hong Kingston, author of
I Love a Broad Margin to My Life

Nothing Left in My Hands:
The Issei of a Rural California Town, 1900-1942
Kazuko Nakane
"*Nothing Left in My Hands* is an engrossing and enlightening story of a California rural community in Watsonville, settled at the turn of the century by Issei immigrants from Japan. Alongside Kazuko Nakane's engaging narrative, the Issei's oral interviews movingly capture the essence of this extraordinary generation—their courage, grit, humor, and character."
—Jeanne Wakatsuki Houston, co-author of *Farewell to Manzanar*
and author of *The Legend of Fire Horse Woman*

The Oracles: My Filipino Grandparents in America
Pati Navalta Poblete
"A tender, funny engrossing memoir."
—Tess Uriza Holthe, author of *When the Elephants Dance*

Journey to Topaz
Yoshiko Uchida, Illustrated by Donald Carrick
In a bleak and dusty prison camp, eleven-year-old Yuki and her family experience true friendship and heart-wrenching tragedy.